The Art-Craft Of Creating Financial Wealth

....

A Migration Experience From Poverty To Riches

Anthony Cepman A. O.

Copyright © 2018 ANTHONY CEPMAN A. O.

All rights reserved.

ISBN-10: 1719484007
ISBN-13: 978-1719484008

DEDICATIONS

I ultimately dedicate this work to God Almighty who gives the power to make wealth and possess riches, and whose will it is for us to be wealthy and live in the realms of prosperity.

To my angel wife and my God sent children, who have always offered me a backbone of strength and encouragement, I dedicate this book.

Also, I sincerely dedicate this work to all the great men and women who are still creating but currently are owners and possessors of financial wealth, and who for their sake of love for humanity have made the right choice to actively engage their wealth and riches for deed of good-works and for rendering of humanitarian services aimed at making positive impact across the world to better the lives of millions of people especially the less privileged and to improve on the development of the society especially the world developing countries and communities.

Such men and women as: Bill Gates; Warren Buffett; George Soros; Azim Pemji; Charles Francis Feeney; Gordon Moore; Eli Broad; George Kaiser; Michael Bloomberg; Paul G. Allen; Mark Zuckerberg; Jon Huntsman; Ted Turner; James Simons; Michael Dell; Pierre Omidyar; Dietmar Hopp; Jeff Bezos; Operah Winfrey; and host of others who are equally bettering the lives of many in their own little way.

ANTHONY CEPMAN A. O.

SYNOPSIS

Abraham Lincoln says, "The best way to predict your future is to create it". The task of creating a predicted future that would become a desired reality is a process. This process requires from you, an art craft of creating a sustainable financial wealth that posterity can share from. Life is worthless if it is not worth living. In destiny is the worth of life. And one of your destiny contents is financial prosperity. Hence, the journey to creating financial wealth must begin with a mastery understanding of financial wealth as a dimension of prosperity which is inseparably connected to your destiny. You should decide to get yourself involved in the art-craft process of creating financial wealth, if you must become financially Independent, Abundant and Able, else you may still be negotiating with poverty in life.

The core motivation for putting up this book is to reverse the choice of many people who have chosen to be poor in life because of the error of their mind that creating financial wealth is a mission impossible. To these people, to be rich in life is a matter of destiny determined by fate and luck. What an infected ideology of the mind!

Why is poverty in the first place? And why are some people poor? Is poverty a phenomenon of creation that originated from God? Does God create some people to be poor and others to be rich? Being poor, is it by fate or a choice? To be poor in life is not by fate but a choice deeply influenced by the lies and deceptions of the mind. Poverty is the act of being poor. And to be poor is a state of financial lack that makes a man unable to afford the basic needs of life namely food, shelter, clothing, and comfort facilities required for daily survival, sustenance and happy living.

To be rich and to create, own and possess financial wealth is an essence for living designed by God for you. Therefore, you must get yourself deeply involved in the art-craft of creating financial wealth, else you may leave behind for your children a legacy of a cycling poverty. Creating financial wealth requires hard-work, determination with focus and self-believe that you can. Accusing your problems as excuses to be poor in life is never acceptable. It is your responsibility to ensure that poverty has no defense to be in your life

To create financial wealth requires a change of poverty-mind-set; it requires a change in one's choices of financial behavior and decision. Your greatest resources to create an empire of financial wealth is in discovering cliental people in whose pockets are money for you to earn; is in finding a value-adding solution to a need in the society; is in exploring investment opportunities to take quick advantage of them before others; is in forfeiting your immediate self-gratification to save up money assets for future investment. God is the giver of life to man, but in poverty a man begins to die and his life becomes tasteless. Creating financial wealth in life is the only guarantee for you to escape poverty with its ugly consequences, which could better be imagined than to be experienced.

Creating financial wealth for yourself is the only option that can empower you with great financial ability to secure your present and future survival and sustenance; to control power to influence people to gain both their allegiance and followership; to position yourself to earn social recognition and honor; to link yourself up to high profile connections and contact to politick your way through in the society; to enjoy preferential rights with personal privileges in the society; and to achieve a self-fulfilled life of greatness.

There is a shackle of generational structure of poverty in the world today that seems to be ruling over many people. You can break this shackle to set yourself free from poverty. It is absolutely possible through financial wealth creation. For a faster creation of financial wealth that would be viable and sustainable, you must choose the profit-earning-driven option of being an employer or hirer of labor who is entitled to earn profit than being an employee or a laborer who works hard for others only to go home at the end with a beggary income pay. Also, you must learn to escape the poverty trap of being a financial liquidator, else you fall into the trap of liquidating your own financial wealth even after creating it.

This book, *"The Art-Craft of Creating Financial Wealth"*, full of great in-demand wealth creation ideas, proven practical business strategies and investment principles is really a product of the author's mastery and experience both as an Investor, Entrepreneur and business investment manager, an Administrator and Management practitioner. Surely, the book is a unique class of its own that has the capacity to empower you to migrate out of poverty into riches. Therefore, if you remain poor, that's your choice. If you become rich, that's your decision. Obviously, no one would be blamed for your poverty. With this book, I assure you that you can rewrite your poverty story, and open for yourself a new chapter of a story book that is full of testimonies of your own financial wealth creation, ownership and possession.

ANTHONY CEPMAN A. O.

CONTENTS

Dedications   v

Synopsis   vi

1. Understanding Destiny   1
2. Understanding Your Destiny Content   19
3. Strategizing Your Destiny Contents With Principles   38
4. Understanding Prosperity   65
5. No Excuses For Being Poor In Life   81
6. Resources For Creating Financial Wealth   99
7. Poverty Is A Choice Not By Fate   117
8. Why You Need To Create Financial Wealth   141
9. Financial Wealth Defines Financial Abilities   152
10. Choices Of Financial Behaviour And Decision   167
11. Requirements For Creating Financial Wealth   186
12. Principles For Creating Financial Wealth 1   196
13. Principles For Creating Financial Wealth 11   226
14. Dare To Become A Hirer Of Labour   251
15. The Other Side Of The Coin Of Financial Wealth   267

CHAPTER ONE

UNDERSTANDING DESTINY

What is Destiny?

Destiny is the strategic resources that God has deposited inside of you. You are a child of destiny. You are a destiny carrier, because you are carrying inside of you a divine strategic resources. No destiny, no birthright from God. Put differently, destiny is your son-ship birthright from God. In fact, God owes and gives you nothing before bringing you into this world other than to give you a destiny. Without destiny you will not be entitled to any claim of son-ship birthright from God as your Father. Destiny is what informed your creation to exist on earth. The vision of you that God has is summed up in your destiny. Your destiny is your God-given bait for survival and greatness. A man without destiny is doomed. It is an error for a man to find himself living on earth with no destiny.

Destiny is the stamp of the creative touch of divinity on a man that launches him out into existence. Destiny is an indication that one is created by God. Anyone without destiny is not from God. For He never creates any man without destiny. Sure, every man created by God and born of a woman whether saved or not saved has a destiny to fulfill. After all, the gift of God is without repentance.

Though how purposeful, complete and well one fulfills one's destiny may be the only issue of concern in relation to salvation. With your destiny you are obviously so rich inside of you. But in the outward of your life you will certainly remain poor as long as you fail to make mastery understanding of your destiny.

The root word, "Destiny" simply stands for: **DAYS OF LIFE; ESSENCE; SELF-ORIGIN; TALENTS; INTENTION; NATURAL WEAKNESS; YEARNING**. The journey to fulfill destiny begins with making a mastery understanding of your destiny. When destiny is masterly understood, fulfilling it becomes possible. And when destiny is in the process of being fulfilled, becoming rich and attaining to greatness in life becomes possible.

D = DAYS OF LIFE

E = ESSENCE FOR LIFE (To Achieve Prosperity)

S = SELF – ORIGIN OF YOU

T = TALENTS OF NATURAL ABILITY TO PERFORM

I = INTENTION TO PURSUE A CAREER DREAM

N = NATURAL WEAKNESS FOR DEPENDENCE AND SELF-CONTROL

Y = YEARNING TO MEET A CERTAIN NEED

Therefore destiny can be defined as, "the divinely estimated resources allocated to a man with which God prepares him to survive, achieve prosperity and live purposefully on earth. In other words, it is with destiny that a man is prepared by God to become great in life".

"Destiny is the creation blue-print of a man's tenure of life (days of life); of why he is here on earth (essence); of who he is (origin); of what he is capable of doing (talents); of which career to pursue in life (intention); of how he is a human (weakness); and of where his interest lies in life (yearning); with all sealed together to prepare you to survive and to live an accountable purpose fulfilling life on earth".

Destiny is a greatness factor. Destiny is the greatest tool of preparation to achieve greatness that God had proposed to man. Therefore, without destiny a man is at all neither prepared to achieve a fulfilled life of greatness. Destiny is the determinant factor for a man's greatness in life. Now ask yourself, have I attained greatness in life? Am I on course to achieve a fulfilled life of greatness? Without making a mastery of your destiny, it is absolutely a mission impossible to achieve a fulfilled life of greatness.

A fulfilled life of greatness is the achievement of the four dimensions of prosperity, the essence for life namely Eternal Life; Sound Health; Financial Wealth; Successful Marriage; and a Legacy as the ultimate and meaningful mission for a man's living here on earth of which destiny is the determinant factor.

Your destiny is a great good work that God had begun and already finished for you in Christ Jesus *(Ph.1v6)*. Therefore you are now only beginning to fulfill what God had already ended for you. And since God had ended what you are now to begin, it means He will definitely be by your side to lead, guide and direct you on how to fulfill your destiny. He won't allow you to end up unfulfilled in life. Having gone ahead of you He knows where there will be dangers, challenges and difficulties. He won't leave you alone. He will surely be with you at those points and seasons within the entire space of time that you would live to fulfill your destiny. He will be there all along to see you through in your journey of fulfilling your great destiny. You cannot fail on the way. Just take a decision of faith today to begin to fulfill your destiny from God's End of it *(Is.46v10)*.

Applying scripture to define Destiny

Destiny is the divine estimation **of all things (resources) allocated to you that pertain to life and godliness** *(2Pet.1v3)*. Going by this definition, it implies that one without destiny has no chance of living a fulfilled life. And without destiny one may lack the potential to live a godly life. Hence, if destiny is the divine estimation of all things allocated to a man that pertain to life and godliness, then without destiny a man may not be able to achieve all the dimensions of prosperity since they have diagonal combination of earthly living for enjoyment and godliness for eternity in heaven. The first three contents of destiny; your days of life, your essence and your self-origin pins you down to the consciousness of godliness – godly living. While that of your talent, intent, natural weakness, and yearning become useful tools with which you will be able to make achievements that brings fulfillment and enjoyment to your life here on earth.

Destiny begins in the Womb

"Before I formed you in the womb I knew you; Before you were born I sanctified you, I ordained (destined) you a prophet to the nations" (Jer.1v5). God is saying to Jeremiah, right at your conception in the womb I have allocated an estimated resources of all things to you that it would take you to be a prophet to the nations.

Omniscient knowledge is the foreknowledge of God. Predestination is a function of this foreknowledge, for that is what makes it possible. Therefore, predestination is the act of demonstration of God's ability to use His foreknowledge to determine the destiny of a man (Is.46v10).

The reality of predestination begins in one's life at the point of conception or formation in the womb (fertilization of the ovary) but prior to one's birth. God knew you before your conception or formation in the womb; and upon your conception He destined you; and upon your birth, you were delivered on earth as a person already prepared to achieve greatness *(Jer.1v4)*. With this reality, one prior to one's birth becomes destined.

Allocation of divinely estimated resources

At every location there is always a releasing of allocation of resources. God chose the earth as your location for dwelling. For this reason He has given you a great destiny as your own portion of resource allocation. This resource allocation is expressly divine without any iota of human determination. You are created a unique person with a customized resource allocation released to you from God. The Almighty God, your loving and caring Father has allocated to you a destiny that is best for you: a numbered days of life to live; an essence for living; talents to perform; intent for a career to earn a living; natural weakness to manage as a human; and yearning to meet a need.

Needless to wonder why David had to say that his own portion of destiny allocation has fallen at pleasant places. If your destiny allocation had come from man, they would have been tampered with. Whatever is divine is beyond human reach. Your destiny is beyond the reach of any man. And because your destiny is divine, it is equally not estimable by human. Your destiny is a hidden treasure and a secret unknown to men. It is a mystery that only God knows. He alone can interpret it and reveal it into reality to amaze the onlookers. Never mind those waiting to see what your life becomes. Know this, your destiny is far from human estimation. **Your destiny is written in the language of the Spirit with the ink of the blood of the Lamb on the golden paper of the spoken Word of God.** Hence, no man or any power can rewrite or change your destiny.

According to *Oxford Advanced Learner's Dictionary*, estimation means a judgment or opinion about the value or quality of somebody or something. People sometimes in their own judgment or opinion do try to estimate or value what they think that you are or would only amount to in life. Their estimation of you many a time determines how they do see you, take you, treat you, relate with you, respect you, react to you and even behave toward you.

All these manners would always be positive from people if in their judgment they think that you are of a high estimation (value) or would become great in life, may be in future. Otherwise, people in their manner of human nature would always regard you as a nobody, a useless somebody, a nonentity, a good for nothing fellow, a barren stock, a minus one, a failure, a liability, a prostitute, a drunkard, a hopeless parasite, a vagabond, a rogue, an unproductive consumer, a head-count human being without a future, a man of Nazareth from whom nothing good would come out, etc.

With this unfair conclusive mindset and judgment, people including those you might lest expect would always be left with no option than to neglect, reject, avoid, abandon or despise you. Why have they chosen to do this? Simply because in their own opinion and judgment they could not see any hope or future in you and could not understand the fact that God has created and predestined you to fulfill a loaded destiny that is higher than their estimation of you.

May be this is exactly the situation and condition in your life right now. You need not to border okay! Never you accept people's opinion about you but be the one to create an opinion for yourself. *Frederic Klopstock* did say, *"He who has no opinion of his own, but depends on the opinions of others, is a slave"*. You should be a master to your destiny not a slave to it.

It is only God who knows your exact estimation and value for which He has created you *(Math.16v13-17)*. So, don't worry yourself with what people are thinking about you. But worry yourself with what others are not thinking about you that you know you are. Worrying is a total waste of time. It doesn't change anything. All it does is to steal your joy and keep you busy doing nothing. Worrying does not take away tomorrow's troubles; it takes away today's peace. Don't border yourself with what they say, but border yourself with what you should say to them about yourself. What other people think of you shouldn't be your business. Don't be discouraged by what people see in you or may choose to call you. Rather, be encouraged by what God sees in you and whom He says you are.

Jacob saw in Joseph a son with greatness but his brothers could only see in him a dreamer. The Midianite traders could only see in Joseph a slave that is good for a business but Potiphar saw in him a noble servant. Potiphar's wife saw in him a handsome man to date. The prisoners could only see in Joseph a fellow prisoner but God had seen in him a prime minister of Egypt in waiting.

You are not just more than what they think you are, but you would eventually by God's grace become what they never thought you would be in life. Though the present facts of realities in your life right now might be tarrying with their estimation of you, yet that does not in any way still make it to be true. God alone would definitely reveal the true realities of His divine estimation of you. By so doing He would crash out and invalidate those facts of realities that men are using to make wrong estimation of you *(1Cor.2v9)*. I tell you, you've got a pretty-good destiny of glory to fulfill. So you must accept this fate and move forward to prove otherwise to those who thought you would only amount to nothing. It is time for you to arise to prove a point to them that you are created and born to be great other than to be nobody.

Your destiny is not accidental

There is no doubt that prior to your conception while you are still in the loins of your father, God already foreknew you. Under a purposeful supervision, God carefully supervised your father's deposition of his semen into the body of your mother. Of course, out of the millions of deposited sperms battling for fertilization in the womb, God in His foreknowledge of you wonderfully singled you out. And thereon right in the womb, you were fearfully formed by God. He did form you and allocated to certain divinely estimated resources inside of you that you would need to amount to greatness. And creating financial wealth for yourself is one of the routes to attaining greatness in life.

Obviously it is for the sake of your destiny that you were born and are now spared by God to live. In other words, you are not just living with nothing but with a destiny for greatness that justifies your creation. Neither were you born by accident without a destiny. Your creation is not at all an outcome of a random chance. It is rather well calculated by God. You are God's customized creation that is full of great destiny. You are a product of God created out of His divine wisdom that was informed by His foreknowledge. Hence, you become predestined to fulfill a destiny. What a kindness of love from God!

Not alone on the journey of your destiny

"Behold, I am with you and will keep you wherever you go, and will bring you back to this land; for I will not leave you until I have done what I have spoken to you" (Gen.28v15).

Truly you are on the journey of your destiny to achieve the divine essence for which you are created. Your destiny is the land of promise that God has vowed to bring you into, regardless of where you may be right now; the troubles of life you may be facing; the fears and conflicting realities of life you may be battling with; or what people around you may be saying concerning you. Time in its due course will definitely reveal better who you are. We all need our own time to travel our distance. Cheer up! The great good news is that God Himself, the very author and finisher of your destiny is with you on the journey of your destiny. He will keep you, preserve you all through and will never leave you alone to your own mercy until He sees you fulfil your destiny. This was God's assurance to Jacob, and it all came to pass. If God has authored your destiny, be sure that He will finish it up for you.

"And the LORD, He is the One who goes before you. He will be with you. He will not leave you nor forsake you; do not fear nor be dismayed" (Deut.31v8).

Of course the journey of destiny is often rough and touch with the troubles of life, risks in life, and oppositions in life but God as the Mighty One would ever go before and ahead of you to clear the way with victories. Therefore, don't be afraid of the giants on the way to the journey of your destiny, for you will definitely sail and scale through over them because you are not alone.

"Have I not commanded you? Be strong and of good courage; do not be afraid, nor be dismayed, for the LORD your God is with you wherever you go" (Josh.1v9).

In fact, the assurance that you are not alone but with God on the journey of your destiny is enough reason for you to be strong and be of good courage. Knowing that He who created you with a great destiny will stick with you all the way to make sure that your destiny is not left unfulfilled. Always remember that you've not arrived there yet. And that you as an individual has your own set time to arrive into your own promised land of a fulfilled destiny. It is wrong to think that your journey of destiny will be of the same success and at the same time with others of the same age, sex, education, family background, and or location of residence.

Perhaps you are not aware that popcorns are normally fried in the same pot, in the same oil, at the same time, and under the same heat conditions; but they do not all pop at the same time. So, do not get yourself worried about those who are despising or treating you with scorn just because you are yet to excel or succeed in life. For there is time for everything and for everyone. Everyone can't manifest at the same time. But one thing is sure. Your own time to pop up will certainly come at God's appointed time. The most important thing is that you will definitely get to same place of a fulfilled destiny where you will in great wealth and success meet with those who had earlier despised and looked down on you.

In life, some may walk, others may run, but remember the Lord gave the tortoise and the horse the same days to reach Noah's ark. Your journey might be rough and tough but you will definitely get to your destination. Of course there are many ways God can take you through to the destination of a fulfilled destiny in life. He may not take you the same way He took your mother, father, friend or colleague. What matters is that God will take you to the destination of a fulfilled destiny only if you don't give up. Yes, the process may differ; the road may not be the same, yet you will get to your own destination of a fulfilled destiny. All things will work together for your good to lead you to your expected end; only if you can give in yourself to God to perfect your destiny. Stop crying, lamenting, and drowning yourself with tears of pity and fear of what the future holds for you. I assure you that every circumstance and challenge you are passing through now is actually building up for you the castle of greatness that the Lord has preserved for you. The playing match of your destiny has already been decided in your favor.

Set your destiny as a vision to be fulfilled

Vision is a life target of destiny that you commit yourself to achieve in life. Vision is a life goal that you set out to achieve which has the capacity to bring a positive addition to your achievements' profile, impact to the life of others and great pleasure to God. Vision is an image picture of destiny. It is a life target. Vision is a man's greatest ability. A man with no vision has no ability at all to fulfill his destiny let alone becoming successful in life. Nevertheless, from the divine perspective, "**Vision** is the ability to see God's will (What God has ordained for you, created you to become or perfected for you) for you through the access of revelation". God does reveal everyone's destiny in copies of vision.

Vision connects a man to his destiny. Hence, you must conceive and have a life-lasing vision to fulfill your destiny. That is to say, it is necessary to have a vision to which you commit yourself in order to fulfill your destiny. Once a man conceives a life-long vision, it releases inside of him an inner ability to go miles of no limit to fulfill his destiny. *"No man that does not see vision will ever realize any high hope or undertake any high enterprise"- Wilson Woodrow. "The poorest man on earth is not a man without a cent but a man without a vision"-*

unknown. In life, vision cannot fail a man but a man can end up a failure when he fails to live without a vision. For destiny to be fulfilled, it must be consciously pursued as a vision. *For without vision the people cast constraints (Prb.29v18).*

I tell you, vision is God's language of ability for the great achievement of fulfilling destiny. At creation, God made great achievement of divinely embodied purpose because He had visions of what He wanted to accomplish. By vision God made artistry of your destiny and through vision He communicates it to you. It is therefore through vision that we partner with God to fulfill our destiny. When you set your destiny as a vision to be pursued in life, fulfilling every aspect of your destiny becomes possible.

The best things in life are free; the second best are expensive – Unknown. Life itself, right to freedom, and right of choice are obviously the very best things in life that are indeed free. They don't cost you a dime. And one of the second best things that are expensive is vision. Apparently it is so expensive that it is not everyone that can have it. Until you begin to see your destiny as a vision, you may never effectively fulfill your destiny.

Fulfilling your destiny is not an event that you will just attend but a journey that you must begin with a vision. Living without a vision in life is worse than losing your sight. Such a man without a vision in life is apparently lost in life. *"The path to success is to take massive, determined action" – Tony Robbins.* Of course, vision is the most massive and greatest determined action that a man can take in life. Be inspired with a vision to fulfill your own glorious destiny if you must be great in life. You need vision than you need money to fulfill your destiny. Vision gives you strength to take the inevitable risks, to minimize chances of loss, and to overcome obstacles or challenges. Broken vision is the real reason why many people live a broken life. Also, men of broken vision end up with broken destiny.

Of course, vision demands maximum focus if it must be realized. Any vision pursued without adequate focus given to it may end up being shattered half way. Where there is a bridge it normally puts a distance between two sides, one at back and one at front. If one is driving a car and losses sight or focus upon getting on a bridge, such one stands the risk of either head crashing with another oncoming car or swaging beneath the bridge. The implication will obviously be the sudden end of a journey without getting to the targeted destination. You can't fulfill the vision of your destiny if you don't focus your attention on it. *"Whatever you focus your attention upon you give your strength and momentum to"- John Mason.* Your strength and momentum should be given to things, issues, activities, matters and concerns that are of priority to the vision of fulfilling your destiny. Break away from everything that stands in the way of which might be a hindrance to fulfilling your destiny in life.

Hear the wise saying of *Confucius*, *"he who chases two rabbits catches neither"*. If you don't go after what you want, you'll never have it. You cannot desire to fulfill the vision of your destiny, and at the same time put your focus on frivolous things and concerns or activities that apparently has nothing or less to do with the vision of your destiny. Eagles have accurate vision: They have the ability to maintain focus on something as far as 5km away. No matter the obstacles, the eagle will not lose his concentration of focus from the prey until he grabs it. Therefore, maintain focus in life towards fulfilling the vision of your destiny no matter what the obstacles may be; certainly you will succeed at last. I pray you will arrive at the preferred life-target of fulfilling your destiny.

CHAPTER TWO

UNDERSTANDING YOUR DESTINY CONTENT

Same allocation of destiny, but different destiny content

To every man on earth is given the same allocation of destiny – days of life to wisely live; essence for life to be achieved; talents to perform better; intent to pursue a career dream; natural weakness to be controlled; and yearnings to meet a need in life. Yet, no two persons anywhere on earth have the same destiny content. Destiny content differs according to the measure of God's grace upon one's life by which one would be able to achieve a fulfilled life of greatness. That is why everybody will never achieve the same measure of a fulfilled life of greatness.

It is only eternal life as a spiritual dimension of prosperity that God releases the same measure of grace upon everyone that believes in Christ, His Son by which it can be achieved. Hence, any destiny fulfilled gives great pleasure to God and brings glory of praise to Him. Destiny does not just give meaning to life but makes life to become purposeful.

1. Divine Days of life

"The days of lives are…, So teach us to number our days…, Shall follow me all the days of my life" (Ps.90v10, 12, 23v6).

There are clear poofs from the above scriptures that you have a number of divine days to life here on earth. Divine, because these days were calculated and allocated to you by God. And this is the very first content that makes up your destiny. No man is brought forth into the earth to whom certain number of days were not allocated to. You have expiring days of life to live here on earth, so do I have too. The earlier you become conscious of this fact, the better for you. You are duty bound to spend these days wisely - judiciously and usefully. To judiciously spend the number of your days is to do only the right things that are ought to be done and at the right time when they should be done. And to usefully spend your days of life is to positively touch and impact on the lives of others through your own life and through whatever thing else which you do that is good for others, benefiting to humanity and acceptable by God, all to the glory of God's name.

Remember that one day, you would become just a memory in the heart of the people you will leave behind. And how long the memory of you would last after your death would depend on how impact-oriented life that you have lived. If posterity would not remember you for ages long after your earthly departure, then you have obviously lived a very wasted life. How long a man lived is not measured by the longevity of his age, but by the longevity of his memory in the heart of the living and his remembrance by them. So, be guided by the principle of wise numbering of your days to be able to live the best of a good life so that posterity would always remember you even after you are gone to the world beyond. David got this revelation and asked God to teach him how to number his days that he may gain a heart of wisdom.

Note that the expiration of your allocated days of life are unknown to you. Bearing this truth in mind, you can't afford to be a mere spectator. Only standing on the gallery of life watching others advancing on the playing ground of achieving the essence for their lives. Your allocated days of life is too short, yet too long enough that you can spend it to live a wise and useful life. Spend the days of your life to do things that are worthwhile, not things that are wasteful. Don't spend it to do things that are lawful but are useless. You shouldn't belong to the league of those whose existence amounted to wasted days of life.

Make the days of your life count, and let it be meaningful on earth. If at the end of the days of your life, you fail to have achieved the essence for which you were created, then the days of your life has ended up useless, wasted, meaningless, and above all, a tragedy. Hear this, don't complicate life. We won't be here forever. Once your allocated days on earth are over, they are gone forever. Your time is too valuable to be wasted on nonsense. Be wise!

2. *Divine Essence for Life*

God had allocated to you a divine essence for life. The fact that it is allocated to you from God did make it divine. The divine essence for life is the destiny content that points at why you are created by God. It directs you to the purpose for your existence on earth. The divine essence for your life is the 'will' of God according to His eternal purpose for you. Of course, this will of God which is the divine essence for your life is to achieve, live in, and be fulfilled in life with the prosperity experience of having **eternal life,** living in **sound health,** owning and possessing **financial wealth,** enjoying **successful marriage** and living for a **legacy** while here on earth. Remember, you are made by the great God who dwells in eternal prosperity that is revealing and transcending both in heaven and on earth. God really want you to make every required effort to achieve each of this dimensions of prosperity while living your life on earth.

According to Apostle Peter in his second epistle, chapter one, verse four, these are the exceedingly great and precious promises that God prepared to give to you as His child. God is eternally immortal that He equally wants you to have eternal life. God is eternally mighty in power that He can heal you and keep you in sound health. God is eternally the source and owner of all gold and silver of financial wealth as well as omniscience and omnipotent in making financial wealth, so He wants you to create this same financial wealth for yourself. God's relationship with man was eternally designed to be successful – fruitful, productive, and fulfilling for which reason He also wants you to have a successful marriage relationship. Also, the entirety of God's creation are epitome of the greatest legacy that still remain humanly unbeatable.

3. *Divine Self-Origin of you*

Your origination from God through your parents has accorded you two identities namely; your source-identity and your birth-identity. The source-identity which is accorded to you from God is higher than the birth-identity accorded to you through your parents. Your source-identity is divine in nature but your birth-identity is biological in nature. Your source-identity not your birth-identity is the real expression of your self-origin. Your source-identity is the real you; is the person you are. Who you are; is not in your birth-identity. Because your birth-identity is just mere biological data and facts. But your source-identity is the standing and lasting truth and reality of whom you are.

It is therefore whom you are that defines what you become in life. Your birth-identity is not the determinant factor for you to achieve a fulfilled life of greatness. But your source-identity is. All you need to do is to begin investigation to find out who you are. The library centre for your investigative finding should be the Word of God spoken about you as contained in the Holy Scriptures. Your source-identity as enumerated below is the reason for which you are precious in the sight of God *(Is.43v4)* and greatly beloved of God *(Dan.10v19a)*.

You are the greatest of God's creation made exactly in His image, after His likeness (Gen.1v26-27). You are a special treasurer to God (Deut.7v6). You are the only being on earth that is almost equal with an Angel (Ps.8v5). You are a human god begotten by God (Ps.82v6). You are not a mistaken but a divinely orchestrated creature that was fearfully and wonderfully made (Ps.139v14). You are the very apple of God's eyes (Zech.2v8). You are the light and salt of the world (Math.5v13-14). You are the most intimate friend of God (John15v13-15). You are a workmanship of God's craftsmanship (Eph.2v10). You are a chosen generation, a royal priesthood, a holy nation, and His own special person (1Pet.2v9).

Like I said before, your birth-identity is just mere facts and data associated with your biological origination. They basically include among other things, names you bear; ancestral linage; family background; genetic inheritance; your day of birth, month and year; gender; native place;

etc. None of these is a factor to determine whether you will achieve prosperity or not. They only represent your biological data and facts which are basically conveyed on curriculum vitae and other official documents, only for the purpose of records and personal references.

In fact, to agree that your birth-identity is a determinant factor for you to achieve a fulfilled life of greatness will automatically invalidate the Word of God in *(Rom.9v15-16)*. It is not by your birth-identity that you can run or 'will' to achieve the essence for your life - prosperity. It is rather only by God's mercy and grace. For example, you don't have to change your names to be able to achieve a fulfilled life of greatness. Or, if you think you really have to, then what about thousands of people across the globe who did change their names, yet they still could not achieve prosperity or live a fulfilled life of greatness but ended up being poor.

4.   *Divine Talents of natural ability to perform/ do a thing*

There is at least a talent embedded inside of you. Every talent originates from God and that makes it divine. Talent is an inherent endowment or a gift of potential in a man that resourcefully provides him with natural ability to effectively perform certain things or do a vocation; possibly without any acquisition of formal training or education. For example, it is talent that explains why a man can put together a meaningful write up even without acquiring any formal education or training on writing; why one can skilfully make an artful drawing or painting, do furniture or carpentry work without any formal education or training on artistry or art-crafting. That thing you are so much good at doing may be your own talent. Personally I discovered I have the talent to write, and that's why I have been able to put together this great book.

Also, talent can be a nurtured or developed skill acquired over time either through formal education, training or learning. This kind of talent is referred to as the acquired talent. Meanwhile no man's talent is ever compared or measured to be the same with another's. However, it is not true to hold on to the popular belief that all men are born equal but are not equally talented. My opinion rather is that all men are born equal with equal talent of the same capacity but are not of the same kind and measure. This portrays God's act of wisdom, limitlessness, dynamism and diversification. In other words, whatever is your talent, it has the same capacity with that of everyone else's to resourcefully enable you to perform a thing or do a particular vocation better. Your talent is so much in measure in relation with God's grace given to you to enable you achieve prosperity in life, of which financial wealth is one of its dimensions *(Math.25v14-26, Luk.19v12-27, Eph.4v7)*.

5. *Divine Intention to pursue a career dream*

Intention to pursue a career dream as one of the destiny contents answers the question of what area of career do I want to go into for a livelihood, or what career job do I want to do in life to earn a living. In every man there is an in-built intention to pursue a career dream that would always call for his attention. This particular intention is from God. And that's why it is divine. That is what you needed without which you won't be able to create let alone to own and possess financial wealth.

Though dream sometimes is often interchanged to mean vision, yet both are not the same. Vision is more of God and from Him, but dream is more of man and comes from man. Dream is rather any specific goal or target set to be pursued by which to achieve a vision. Vision is an end but dream is the means to achieve the end. You can't achieve a vision until you have a dream to pursue it. Indeed, am sure everyone including you has a vision to achieve the prosperity of financial wealth. Obviously this singular vision of yours, you cannot achieve in life if you have no intention of pursuing any career dream.

Vision, I tell you, is always higher than dream. Vision gives birth to dream. And dream once it is birthed by vision, it becomes a path way to achieving a vision. Dream begins and ends up in achieving a vision. But vision begins and continues to be a life time objective awaiting to be achieved. Right inside of you is a divinely imbedded intention to pursue a particular career dream in life. For example, ask every little child including your own child, what he or she wants to do or become in life. Some may say, doctor, lawyer, musician, pastor, soldier, journalist, footballer, film actor or actress, etc. One may actually wonder if the little children are so sure of what they are saying. Yes, they are in majority of cases. They are saying it because one of their destiny contents called intention to pursue a career dream is apparently revealing itself in them. If little children could have an intention to pursue a career dream, then how much more you that is of older age.

To support the above fact, hear this; *"I can't decide what career path my children will take because God by Himself had already figured that out. I only need to pray that He orders their steps and they are sensitive to His leading while my husband and I guide them rightly. The one thing we have power over is the kind of character we want them to have"* – *An Anonymous Mother.*

You may ask, why is it that God made an intention to pursue a career dream to be one of your destiny content. The answer is obvious. It is because without it you cannot create financial wealth of which is located at the centre of other dimensions of prosperity. You see, money which is a product of creating financial wealth have direct inverse relationship with other dimensions of prosperity. For instance, you need money to get yourself Bible; to get yourself faith-building, lifting and inspiring Christian books, cassettes and video messages that could help you to grow and mature spiritually and to become more fervent in faith; to get yourself transported to the church for daily or weekly fellowship with brethren and to hear God's Word; to fulfil your statutory spiritual obligations (tithing and offerings) and to make other necessary contributions to support God's work. In other words, without money you may struggle to sustain the saving-faith of your soul unto eternal life.

Also, you need money to get yourself the best of medical attention; to get yourself drugs for appropriate treatment; to get good food for yourself to feed on; to make your house conducive enough for you to always have good rest. Without financial wealth, achieving sound health may not be 100% possible. To create financial wealth you need money too as a source, perhaps to go to formal school to acquire education or specialized learning required to secure a career job; to get yourself some educative business and investment books and knowledge impacting wealth creation periodicals, publications, journals, newspapers and or other relevant print materials.

And to achieve a successful marriage, of course you need money, to compliment your love for your spouse no matter how he or she seem to be understanding your feelings of love; to train your children; to provide for your family; and to sustain your marriage besides God's grace. As well, you invariably need money too to achieve immortalized legacy - adding value, bringing benefits and progress to the society during your lifetime that would fetch you an indelible good name of gold in your generation. It is for all these reasons that God had embodied you with an intention to pursue a career dream by which you would be able to earn money and eventually create riches to become wealthy, without which you may not be able to effectively achieve other dimensions of prosperity.

6. *Divine natural weakness for dependence and self-control*

It is evident that there is no perfect man anywhere on earth whom God has created that is not without weakness. You and I do have our unique individual weaknesses. God had made you with such a weakness and allowed you to live with it, therefore He is fully aware of your weakness. That's why it is considered to be divine. On the other hand, it is natural because everyone else like you has his or her own weaknesses. Of course, your weakness does not in any way indicate that God is imperfect or lacks the power to have made you perfect. The answer is no. You are a perfect being created but with weakness as human. Obviously, it is for a purpose that will allow all things that shall happen in your life to work together for your own good as long as you love God *(Rom.8v28)*.

To the best of my knowledge, your natural weakness is designed by God to constantly bring you daily to the point of absolute dependence on God's grace lest you boast in your own strength. Hence the Word of God, *"And He said to me, 'My grace will be sufficient for you, for My strength is made perfect in weaknesses'. Therefore most gladly I will rather boast in my infirmities (weaknesses), that the power of Christ may rest upon me".*

Through your natural weaknesses, God is calling you to the character of self-control (discipline) and to the attitude of dependence on the strength of His grace. Through your weaknesses, God tests your resolve to self-control and for dependence on Him. Apostle Paul had his own natural weaknesses that he had battled with for a long time in his life. His own weaknesses had even grew to become a thorn on his flesh despite the abundance revelations being given to him by God. His weaknesses became a contact point on which Satan was capitalizing and taking advantage of it to buffet him *(Rom.7v19)*. Paul got disturbed and pleaded with God to cause the weaknesses to depart from him. And all God could say was that His grace will be sufficient for him.

Then Paul was so humbled by the answer God gave him that he responded thus, *"Therefore I take pleasure in infirmities (weaknesses)..., for Christ's sake, for when I am weak, then I am strong (in grace)" (2Cor.12v7-10).* With this encounter, Apostle Paul had to learn his lessons that your weaknesses are not designed to be a restriction, but to be a reminder to you that you are a mere human. They are not designed to make you stumble in life, but to make you become strong in God's grace. They are not designed to bring you to destruction but to bring you to dependence on God.

7. Divine Yearnings

Helen Keller once said that *"Life is either a daring adventure or nothing else".* Nothing else releases you into the full adventure of life than your yearnings. In the pursuit of making your destiny a master piece to achieve a fulfilled life of greatness, you must take daring steps to resurrect the yearnings that is divinely deposited inside of you. Whatever thing good you are yearning for is not just ordinary. Such yearnings are not only divinely backed up but also has on them the authority stamp of divinity. Yearning could be so powerful that it prevails even in the face of all odds, limitations and or oppositions. Yearning provokes desire to attract divine assistance. Desire generates passion. Passion stirs up interest. Interest leads to attention. And attention meets need to bring satisfaction. There is a need which you can meet, but you have to be fully equipped with a yearning or passion for it. Everyone who has a yearning easily discovers a solution to a need. Run with passion and an infectious enthusiasm and let it find expression in the work of your hands.

Of course when you give attention to a thing, you get an attainment of something. Yearning is that desire that is popping up in you day in, day out which you wouldn't let go away. Desire is that thing you are passionate to achieve or have in life. Passion is that burning interest in you that you are daily consumed with. Interest is that thing you give total attention to with every of your effort and resources. The power of yearning brings with it bravery and gut. You are either a man of bravery and gut or you live to wallow in the stinking gutters of life. Someone said that bravery is the only cure to slavery. Hence, you must discover and pursue your yearnings else you may live in slavery all through your life.

Discovering your own destiny

Remember, Destiny is the allocation of divinely estimated resources that are strategic to you. Without the quest to advance towards creating riches to become wealthy in life, you may never embark on the discovery of your destiny. And without making discovery of your destiny, you may never be inspired to overtake others in measures of creating financial wealth in life. The greatest discovery you can make for yourself in life is the discovery of your destiny. Ordinarily as a Christian, it would be a difficult task for you to discover your destiny outside God's Word and the Holy Spirit.

"But God has revealed them to us through His Spirit, for the spirit searches all things, yes, the deep things of God... Now we have received... the Spirit who is from God, that we might know the things that have been freely given to us by God" (1 Cor. 2v10-12).

Considering the above Bible passage, it is clearly evident that the Word of God is the sole source from which God through His Spirit has always revealed the destiny of man to him. The truth is that God is the author and master of every man's destiny. You can only discover your destiny from God's Word and through the Holy Spirit who has the mastery of your destiny. Every of the contents of your destiny does not only has a root base in the Word of God but also is in agreement with it. Obviously, based on the knowledge of the Word of God from Genesis to Revelation, there is a revelation truth and understanding that every man has only but a few number of days to live; is living for a purpose; endowed with natural talents; designed with an intention to engage in a career work; has an inherent human weakness; and has burning yearnings to always meet a certain need in life.

Typically, Jesus too as a Son of man, lived only but for 33years of a righteously focused, minded and patterned life after His father.

Christ's essence of living was for the purpose of bringing

salvation to all men so as to restore man back to his lost prosperity - of eternal life for which He died and shed His blood on the cross; sound health for which He took our infirmities and bored our sickness; financial wealth for which reason He became poor for us; successful marriage relationship between man and woman as exemplified in the eternal union between Christ and the church, all for the purpose of achieving and leaving behind a life-outliving legacy of supernatural manifestations – uncommon miracles and unusual signs with great wonders.

Christ was naturally endowed with talents of teaching and of making uncommon speeches – full of words of wisdom and knowledge, proverbs and parables.

Christ's career intention was to be a saving Lord, an advocating judge and interceding High Priest of God forever.

Christ has no weakness of human nature because He was not human even though He lived in the human form so as to be in position to sympathize with us in our own weakness.

Christ's yearning and desire according to Peter's report was to passionately meet the only one thing of doing good to all and healing (setting free) all who were oppressed by devil *(Acts10v38)*.

Also, Apostle Paul too lived a focused, minded and patterned life after Christ and died after the expiration of the number of days or years allocated to him.

Paul achieved prosperity as the essence for his living (through faith in Christ he responded to God's call for the salvation of his soul unto eternal life, he lived in unfailing sound health, he was never poor but was so rich in financial wealth at least to be able to meet his basic needs and to share with others, though not married yet he had a successful marriage union with Christ, and he left a life-outliving legacy of spiritual impartations and doctrinal teachings of all time).

Paul made productive use of his talent of tent making and different spiritual gifts.

Paul after he had realized that it wasn't God's original intention for him to pursue a legal career did make a reverse immediately and pursued God's intention of a career for him to become an apostolic minister of the gospel of Christ.

Paul never lived without having to struggle with his own inherent natural human weakness *(Rom.7v13-25)*.

Paul's utmost yearning and desire was to meet the only one need of preaching Christ crucified and to bear witness of the risen Christ as the Son of God and savior of all mankind.

Now that you have clearly understood your destiny contents, you must right away begin to make a mastery of each of them if at all you really want to achieve a fulfilled life of greatness beyond your equals.

CHAPTER THREE

STRATEGIZING YOUR DESTINY CONTENTS WITH PRINCIPLES

Truly, you need proving principles to strategize each of your destiny content. To strategize your destiny content is to right-track your life towards the direction of achieving your life-essence for living - prosperity. Each of your destiny content requires a particular principle by which it can be strategized namely as follows;

Your days of life – Apply the principle of numbering your days for a life hereafter

According to David, to number the days of your life with a heart of wisdom simply requires that you live your life objectively and consciously to stand righteous both before God and men while you are here on earth so as to inherit the life hereafter.

Therefore, to number your days for the life hereafter is to live a life that is patterned and shaped by God's Word. It is all about living a life that its end would produce an immortalized testimony of **righteous relationship with God and men, selfless deed of good works and positive impact on others, and good use of your God given resources namely; talent, money, time, brain.**

These in the sight of God are more profitable than to have an empire of financial wealth which perishes thereafter.

Also, to number the days of your life is to live a righteous and upright life; it is to live a purpose oriented life; it is to live at the centre of obedience to God's Word; it is to live a life of positive impact; it is to live for others; it is to live an error-free life; it is to live an emulative and exemplary life; it is to live with a hope of hereafter, etc. Hence you should not allow anyone to distract, interrupt and obstruct you from numbering the days of your life objectively and consciously. Never should you allow those who are making waste of their days of life to entice and influence you to do same, lest they make your own days of life here on earth to become meaningless, useless and without reward of the hope of eternal glory.

Those who never numbered the days of their lives wisely, not only died and were forgotten here on earth but shall also lose the eternity of life that is to come. But those whose lives and living were shaped and patterned by God's Word, died and their names lives on. And they are ever celebrated by posterity. All because of their righteous relationship with fellow men, selfless deed of good works and positive impact, as well as judicious use of their talents. You must get yourself ready to continually make wise numbering and spending of the days of your life. Applying the principle of numbering the days of your life is not negotiable if you want to make the best out of your living while still on earth. Remember life is short, don't break the rules; forgive quickly, love truly, and give yourself to every act that makes you righteous and worthy before God.

Your essence for living – Apply the principle of Determination

One of the hardest decision you will ever face in life is choosing whether to walk away or to try harder one more time. That's determination! The choice is yours but remember you can't fall if you don't climb, though there is no joy in living your whole life on ground – *Anonymous*. Know this, a stone is broken by the last stroke of hammer but that doesn't mean that the first stroke is useless. Therefore, creating a lifelong financial wealth would always require determination with a continuous effort. Never stop until you achieve your vision of creating financial wealth as a dimension of prosperity. Yield to the hands of determination. If you stay on track and remain determined, you will find success at the end of the road. Even when your vision seems impossible to reach, determine to try anyway. You will be amazed by what you can accomplish.

Determination I will say is the force of an inner drive or motivation that generates inside of you a resolute and striving will, courage and strength to achieve a worthwhile goal despite all surrounding odds, limitations, fears, challenges, threats, and problems.

In particular, such odds, limitations, fears, threats, challenges and problems that one usually face in life while attempting to achieve ones essence for living may cut across spiritual, health, psychological, financial, marital, and condition of the social environment.

You need determination, if you must achieve prosperity – eternal life, sound health, financial wealth, successful marriage, and legacy as the very essence of why you are here on earth. Determination will birth in you the strength to create financial wealth and to be able to fully live in riches. With determination one continues to have hope at every stage in one's life. When determination births hope; with hope you see a picture of reality that future holds for you. When Job began to allow discouragement to sink down his determination to survive his situation, he could no longer see any hope of himself living again in sound health and becoming owner and possessor of financial wealth *(Job7v6-7)*.

The power of determination is the force that arrests your mind and compels you to say "yes I can". When the force of determination grips hold of you, it creates in you an image mirror through which you see possibilities. Impossibility is an enemy of determination. Determination brings you to the abode of possibility. And when determination and possibility meets together, a new reality is created. When the force of determination took over Paul, then after he says, *"I press toward the goal (to achieve the essence for his living) for the prize of the upward call of God in Christ" (Ph.3v14)*. The upward call of God in Christ for Paul was to achieve prosperity besides fulfilling his ministry, which he eventually achieved. Even though he never married, but he was in covenant union with Christ, hence his marriage union with Christ was successful.

Determination can do inside of you what you wouldn't imagine. Determination beats imaginations especially when the force of its current is wired inside of you. In the face of great famine and financial crunch, with determination the four hopeless, dejected, ostracized, neglected, abandoned, disrespected, rejected and despised lepers at the entrance gate of the city of Samaria made history and became heroes just in one day *(2Kg.7v3-16)*. Determination made them change their ugly poverty status just overnight. They assumed a new lift of status that moved them from being **native lepers** to becoming **national leaders**, who led the entire nation of Israel to the camp of survival, abundance and satisfaction. Determination took them to a new national appointment of honor, from **leprosy-deformed** to **licensed-informants** to the national executive council. With determination, their positions were changed from **public outcasts** to **patriotic heroes**. *"It* *takes a heart to make a mark"- David Oyedepo.* I guess, that must be a heart of determination. Determination is exactly what you need for you to create financial wealth and become rich as a dimension of prosperity which is the very essence for your living here on earth.

"Nothing in the world can take the place of determination. Persistence and determination alone are omnipotent" – *Calvin Coolidge.* Determination is a prima-facia evidence of readiness to do a thing despite whatever obvious challenges or odds to be faced. Demonstrate yours today and nothing can stop you from achieving prosperity which is inclusive of wealth and riches. Remember, when you consecrate your life to a cause, failure becomes impossible. Don't forget, it took Solomon a great determination to achieve the great success of building a magnificent, famous and glorious temple of Jerusalem *(2Chr.2v1)*. Believe me, you have a magnificent, famous and glorious essence for living. And one of them is to create, own and possess financial wealth of your own. Spur yourself up with a great determination to achieve this feat.

No matter what knocks you down in life, get up and keep going. Never give up, for nothing great is achieved in life without determination and perseverance. Good things could come to those who believe; better things could come to those who are patient; and the best thing would certainly come to those who don't give up. You see, being defeated is often a temporary condition; but giving up is what makes it permanent. Hold on with determination, and you will get there at the destination of achieving prosperity.

Your self-origin – Apply the principle of Self-believe

Believing in yourself is the first secret to the success of being yourself. Don't compare your life to others. You have no idea what their journey is all about. Sometimes you think, if I could just be like so-and-so person, I do be happy. When you compare yourself with other people you are asking for fake. There is only one person you should strive to be; and that's yourself. When you try to imitate another person and act like him, invariably you end up depressed and frustrated. You need to be honest with yourself, be who you are. People you compare yourself with may be weak in the areas where you are strong, and vice versa.

Remember, your real self is in your source-identity not in your birth-identity. Self-believe is the key principle with which to strategize your destiny content of self-origin. You must firmly believe in your source-identity which defines who you are. The greatest strength of yourself lies in your self-believe. Self-believe is the act of believing in yourself firmly. Obama of America, by his re-echoing of the words, "I can and we can" during his first tenure campaign speeches did roll out a declaration of his self-believe to build a greater America together in partnership with all Americans. Why? Because he so much believed in who he is, and who he has become over the years. With a convincing knowledge of who he is, he had the self-believe that he can rule America as her first black president. And he eventually did. If Obama could demonstrate such a high self-believe, how much more you who in Christ has a mind blowing source-identity.

Henry Ford once said, *"If you think you can or think you can't, you are right".* That is to say, 'you can or can't is a factor of self-believe. In fact, self-believe is an attitude that you must cultivate inside of you. Nothing stops you when people don't believe in you but everything stops you when you don't believe in yourself. *"The only thing that stands between a man and what he aims in life is often merely the will to try and the faith to believe that it is possible"- Richard M. Devos.* Your self-believe must always precede your will to try, and your faith to believe in anything else.

Someone says, "The moment you doubt whether you can do something, you cease forever to be able to do it. Don't be afraid to feel uncomfortable. Don't be afraid to look uneasy and little silly in front of others. It's all about your commitment to learning and growing. Decide that your essence for living is far more important than your self-imposed limitations. Dare to try! Step outside of your comfort zone... Believe you can and you are halfway there".

To build yourself-believe, you must deal with and work on your obvious weakness, negative habits, attitudes and behaviors so as to lift your self-esteem and personality-face. Add greater value to your life and enhance your personal confidence through mentorship and coaching. Through inspirational and motivational books grow your drive, motivation and inspiration to believe in yourself so as to hold on to your vision or to pursue a new one. Also, you must deal with your inner self-doubt. Your inner self-doubt takes away your self-believing ability and leaves you with fear. Fear takes away your inner peace and security, and leaves you with worry. And worry takes away your inner relaxation and leaves you with outward anxiety and panic over life.

You should roll yourself up to look inside-inward to believe in yourself and just say to yourself, "I can". With this confession of self-believe, you will be able to do away with inferiority complex and self-effacing. Without doing this you will still be facing the ugly challenge of struggling to develop for yourself the positive self-conception and self-esteem that you needed to stand out in life. *Venus Williams* the lawn tennis heroine once said, *"You have to believe in yourself when no one else does"*. If you must make any headway in life, then you should have inside of you a resolved positive believe in yourself.

Your talents – Apply the principle of Discovering, Developing and Engaging

Inside of you is great resource and treasure of talent yet to be discovered, fully tapped and adequately engaged into effective use. This deposited talent inside of you is designed to be profitable to you as well as to enhance your performance ability in life *(Math.25v14-30)*. The greatest tragedy of all time that can happen in your life is for you to live and die without discovering, developing and effectively engaging your talent into meaningful use. Unlike the unprofitable lazy servant who went and buried his own talents, you shouldn't do same. Making a good investment of your own talent can only begin with discovering, developing and engaging it into use.

Basically, besides the acquired talent (knowledge and skills) through formal education, training or learning, there are three categories of talents namely; Mind talents (creative thinking, intelligence and sensitivity); Spiritual Talents (various gifts of the Spirit); Skilful Talents (craft and art) *(Exd.36v1)*. Yours own talent is lying inside of you waiting for you to discover, develop, and engage them into appropriate use. Sure, this is what *Ralph Waldo Emerson* meant when he says, *"what lies behind us and what lies ahead of us are tiny matters compared to what lies within us"*. If you don't discover, develop and engage your talent that lie inside of you; then you may not recover what lies behind you; and may not get what lies ahead of you.

In rich proportion, your talent is lying right inside of you. Dig them out to discover them. Your talent have the capacity to get you out from behind to the forefront in life. You really have to discover and develop your innate talent, and engage them into most profitable use, together with your acquired talent. It is either you discover your talent or you cover your talent for waste. It is either you develop your talent or you envelop your talent with redundancy. It is either you engage your talent into use or you engineer your talent into dormancy. Men who fail to discover, develop and engage their own talents become imitators of others who discovered, developed and are profitably engaging theirs into use.

Don't forget, imitation is tragic. And the tragedy of imitating someone else is that it lands you into limitation and complication. Hence, you become exposed as fake. And fake can only fetch you failure in life. *Bishop T. D. Jakes* once says, *"You can imitate me but still you can't be me"*. It is only acceptable to imitate ones good works *(1Thes.2v14)* and emulate ones good life but not at all to imitate the usage of another man's talent. It can be suicidal and may amount to an effort in futility. It is so risky that you can even break down half way or get confused and become frustrated. Discovering, developing and engaging your own talent into profitable use brings you to the world of great originality, productivity and personality. Strive to get yourself into this world where it becomes easier for you to create financial wealth and live a rich person.

Your intention to pursue a career dream – Apply the principle of Action-plan with Focus

Your career dream is the career job that you set out to pursue in life which you intend to engage yourself into in order to be earning income for a livelihood or for the purpose of rendering selfless service. By God's design, your intention to pursue a career dream would always has a connecting link with your yearning in life to meet a need in the society. These two destiny contents do have direct relationship with each other. Therefore, whatever is the career dream that you intend to pursue in life should be in tandem or agreement with your yearning in life. For example, if your yearning is to give life to others, care for their health and well-being of their body, it would be right if your intention to pursue a career dream is actually getting you focused on becoming either a doctor, nurse, pharmacist, medical laboratory scientist, medical physiologist, medical physiotherapist, etc.

Whatever or whichever career dream you intend to pursue in life, be sure to have a well spelt out action-plan by which it will be achieved. Else, your career dream may end up becoming a nightmare instead of a reality. Depending on the career dream you intend to pursue, your action-plan to achieve it may either be any of these or all: to acquire formal education or learning; to acquire apprenticeship training; to undergo skill acquisition training; to acquire trade learning experience, etc. It is through your action-plan to achieve your career dream that you get the relevant qualification needed to either perform or do your intended career job.

If your career dream is such that requires you to acquire formal university education; the choice of your course of study must wisely be made in view of your career dream. You must not choose a course of study that is not relevant and appropriate for your set career dream. Also, if your career dream is to go into such career jobs as motor mechanic operator, vehicle driver, motor panel beater, bicycle repairer, hair-dresser, tailor, barber or electrician, I guess the right action-plan to achieve it is to acquire or undergo an apprenticeship, skill acquisition or technical college training in the area that is relevant to the particular career job of your interest.

Or if your career dream is to go into business as a career job; the right action-plan to achieve it is to acquire a formal trade and or business learning experience that is relevant to the particular area of business or trade of your interest, such as - importation, wholesaling or retailing in home appliances, cosmetics, beverages, textiles and clothing, vegetable and fruits, food stuffs, general articles, building materials, etc. *"Every individual has a place to fill in the world and it is important, in some respect, whether he chooses to be so or not" – Nathaniel Hawthorne.* It is your career dream that takes you to a career job where best you can fit in, in life.

Often than not, the career dream of many is broken by loss of focus. Life is so much brighter when we focus on what truly matters. To focus means to concentrate your effort, time, energy, and resources to enforce an action plan towards achieving a set goal or dream. When focus is lost, the passionate commitment to pursue your career dream is also lost. You must be driven by focus to remain on the direction of pursuing your career dream. You must maintain your focus-driven energy, else you lose the strength to achieve your career dream. When you lose focus, diminishing return sets in to crumble your efforts to achieve your career dream. Be ever focused in your pursuit to achieve your career dream. Anyone without focus will always stop by to throw stones at every dog that barks on his or her way, and never will he get to his or her dream destination.

Hear the wise saying of *Henry Kaiser,* *"Determine what you want more than anything else (figure out a career dream) in life, write down the means by which you intend to attain it (roll out your action-*

plan) and permit nothing to deter you from pursuing it (maintain a motion of focus)". Don't allow pleasure to breakdown your focus to achieve your career dream. *"Only those who stay focused on their task end up as front-liners"* – David Oyedepo. If you allow your focus to achieve your career dream to be broken, you may never be able to create financial wealth but may end up a poor man *(Prb.21v17)*. Every of your time is valuable.

Therefore, you should focus on spending your valuable time to do things that are reasonably beneficial and worthwhile to your career dream. You shouldn't concentrate on engaging yourself in activities and or doing things that are not relevant, needful and useful to your career dream *(1Cor.10v23)*. Concentration determines outcomes. Therefore, don't allow those things that matter most in your life to be at the mercy of activities that matter the least. Focus on making the most efficient of your time to engage yourself in things that could add more value to your life. If you don't sacrifice for what you want, what you want will be the sacrifice. Because I know what I want and wouldn't want it to be sacrificed for what I don't want, I had for seven years now stopped watching movies or spending much of my valuable time on television than necessary except for news and at my set leisure time when I do watch football to relax myself.

Make sure at every point of your leisure time you are

reading a book that is either related to your career dream or capable of enhancing your performance in doing your career job. If you spend 20 minutes reading daily, for 52 weeks you would have consumed 1,000,000 words. As much as possible, stay away from television. You can watch educational channels that would benefit you. Men with big TV do sit in front of them to watch men with big library. These categories of men you spend time to watch do not come from the superhuman-planet but are ordinary men like you. The difference is that they have added value to their life; built an attractive career performance that have made them a star for you to watch. You can be one of them if you choose to spend your time adding more value to yourself than sitting all day watching them on TV.

For instance, it is a loss of concentration if your career dream is to become a doctor, and you are spending your valuable time watching movies as if you want to become an actor or actress. You need not to be spending more of your time making an artistic work as if you want to become an artist whereas your career dream is to become a journalist. You need not to be spending your time all day on computer as if you want to become a computer operator or engineer whereas your career dream is to become a footballer. You need not to be spending more of your time travelling here and there as if you want to become a journalist whereas your career dream is to become a teacher. You need not to be spending your time fasting and praying all day as if you want to become a pastor whereas your career dream is to become a businessman. To be concentrated requires that you should prioritize your time only on activities that are most related and useful to your career dream.

Tim Redmond understood this fact when he said, *"There are many things that will catch my eyes, but there are only a very few that catch my heart… It is those I consider to pursue". "With over five hundred television channels, billions of web pages and instant messaging, not only does our whole society suffer from information overload but also our today's youths are consequently suffering from a glut of too many choices other than the choice to be focus toward achieving success in life" (Paraphrased) – Don Daniel Ortiz.* Unfortunately, we are living in a world that is full of diverse tempting pleasures - discoveries and inventions that appear so enticing and inviting to its teaming inhabitants, only but to their own detriment, destruction and above all, loss of concentration.

Most of those irrelevant and un-useful things that can catch your eyes and attention may distract, derail, interrupt and obstruct your concentration to pursue your career dream to achieve it. Beware of loss of concentration to frivolities. For, *"we are what we repeatedly do"- Aristotle.* Come out today from the dungeon of distractions to become concentrated enough to be able to make your career dream a reality. Don't lose concentration by the ever incoming vehicles of distractions, else you may be hit hard by it. Should you allow this to happen to you, tragically you will crash in your pursuit to achieve your career dream.

Your Natural weakness – Apply the principle of Dependence and Self-control

God is aware that He had created you with a self that is weak, of which He requires you to control and to depend on Him for the strength of His grace. No man is living who is not with a trace of an inherent weakness that is evident in his live. Natural weakness in man is a divine assignment given to man to manage all through his life on earth. They are only meant to remind you that you are human, and not to prove your vulnerability. That particular weakness in you is eventually what has become an instrument through which God tests your character of self-control and your attitude of dependence on Him.

To develop the character of self-control is not automatic. It is not by imitation but by intimation with discipline. It only requires you to constantly work on your weakness with discipline until you have built a life-line strength or stamina that will always keep your weaknesses and inferiorities under a subduing check. Otherwise if you don't manage your life through self-control to subdue your weak **self**, your weaknesses and the self in you may subdue you to a standstill in life. And it can limit you from achieving the prosperity of financial wealth. Self-control in little things will give a significant dominion over great things. Also, self-control over unhelpful things will give a sizeable control over reputable things.

Yes, working on yourself may seem the hardest part of life. Yet continue to work on yourself to keep growing up no matter at the level you are. Attend seminars and training on any area you need to improve yourself. Yet, pointing on the need for one to work on one's self-weakness, *Harry S. Truman* says, *"In reading the lives of great men, I found that the first victory they won was over themselves".* Yes, a man's weakness becomes his greatest limitation in life if he fails to work with discipline on his prevalent natural weakness. Remember, your bad habits are your greatest liabilities in life.

Any ship in history that has ever anchored at the bay of its destination was navigated by a captain. You should learn to become the captain of yourself, if you must safely navigate over and through your natural weakness. Else you may lack the strength and stamina to anchor yourself at the bay of your destination in life. To self-control your weakness requires that you continually work on yourself with discipline until you bring your weakness to a total check, to subdue and rule over it. This is the navigation instrument that you all need in life to land yourself on the shores of greatness. Even Apostle Paul had to navigate over and through his own natural weakness by working on his own weakness with discipline *(1Cor.9v27)*. Until you build a lifeline strength and stamina over your weakness, you may not be able in life to self-control it.

However, no matter the level or extent of discipline with which you are working on your weakness, you still need to absolutely depend on God for the strength of His grace to live above your weakness. Otherwise the grace of God would be invalidated by your own works so to say, hence it becomes of no effect but in vain upon your life *(Eph.2v8-9, 1Cor.15v9-10)*. Therefore, you need God's grace on daily basis, the undeserved help of God from God to overcome your weakness. And that's why you must completely depend on God for the daily release of His grace upon you. When grace rests upon you, weakness wearies out. When grace rests upon you strength is made manifest in your weakness.

Nothing else may be sufficient in your life but the grace of God is much more exceedingly sufficient and abundantly available for you *(Eph.2v7)*. You can have it in your life if you care to and desire for it. It is limitless and inexhaustible. Even the sinners by God's mercies do enjoy certain level of it let alone you who is a child of God *(Rom.6v1, Tit.3v11)*. Meanwhile, the fact is that in the matter of managing your weakness, you don't need certain level of God's grace but the fullness of it.

Without grace, the undeserved help of divinity reserved for you in Christ, you may not be able to live above your weakness. You need it and you are really qualified to get it. Only what you need to do if you have been lacking God's grace in your life is to declare your absolute dependence on God. Christ is full of grace and in Him grace has now appeared to all men including you by which you can now only by it be saved from your weakness. Yes, grace is available but never affordable without your salvation *(Rom.6v1)*. Of course the decision is yours. You can be wise to decide today for your salvation by accepting Christ as your Lord and Savior, in order to activate God's grace to be able to overcome your weakness.

Yearning – Apply the principle of Desire with Passion

There's no person passionate that fails. Until you desire in life to create financial wealth for you to live in riches; until you put great interest in your effort to achieve it; until you have passion to achieve it; and until you become consumed with yearning to achieve it; you never can have it in life.

A Nigerian man by name, Larry Izamoje simply enjoys talking sports! From very rough and tough days as a child on the streets of Warri in Delta State, Nigeria. As a young graduate he struggled hard in order to put food on the table. With his determination to become a successful media entrepreneur he followed hard his yearning for analyzing and reporting sports. This later paid off when he eventually establish 88.9 Brila FM, a trail blazing, all-sports radio station (the first in Nigeria) which is fast becoming a remarkable and highly relevant player in Nigeria's sports information sector. His example shows us the many advantages of finding what one is passionate about and building a business around it and working with fun!'

Desire is the nucleus of creativity. *Napoleon Hill* said *"Desire and achievement is the starting point of all achievements"*. Yearning stimulates creativity and achievement when coupled with passionate action. It puts the law of cause and effect into motion. Your yearning will literally determine your destiny. Or should I say that what you do that you yearn for will literally determine your destiny. It is the fire of yearning that fuels your intensity of purpose. A person with a burning desire to achieve a goal of any kind is automatically driven towards it. Desire is the fuel in the furnace of ambition and the power in your personality. The primary reason most people don't achieve a fulfilled life of greatness is that they are not passionate enough about what it is that they want to be, have or do in their life. They simply do not desire it enough.

The only way you can acquire an intensive burning desire for a monthly goal is for that goal to be aligned with your time and highest values. Desire and passion are the tools that can allow your reality to work; but desire and passion do not have to be expressed in a struggle type of mode. Desire is the activation key that will bring to a real life experience anything you believe to be possible in life. When you allow your desire and excitement, which is an indication of your connection to the primal energy out of which all is created. And when you allow your desire to bring those things into your life, then your life will be effortless and miraculous day by day. Bashes S.E's comment on desire is quite interesting: *"What is typically called a miracle is in actual fact recognition of the fundamental markings of the universe".*

So, if you wish your life to become more and more an effortless expression of that level of creativity, then all you need to do is allow your life to revert back to its natural state, the zero-rest balance point; to allow the things in your life to be there that need to be there, rather than thinking you must make, force or push those ideas into creation. *"Lord, grant that I may always desire more that I can accomplish"*- Michelangelo. A great philosopher once observed that, "Naked I see the camp of those who desire nothing." You must cultivate a strong sense of longing for a worthwhile existence. This is purely about your expectation level, your ability to desire something strongly and with great emotion.

You must have lofty ambitions and strong predisposition to greatness. I call it the longing to make a difference, the drive to make an impact in life. No man was sent to earth by God to end up a mere speck on life's horizon. You must have dreams to meet certain needs of others that you yearn so much for and desired so much to achieve. And they must be big dreams that you have burning passion for. Something special is that inexplicable feverishness at your heart that just won't go away.

The name 'Cepman' which I now bear is born out of my revealing YEARNING to be a crusader of equal privileges to every man (CEPMAN). This particular yearning was my motivation to establish a Christian based Non-Governmental Organization (NGO), through which I am reaching out to save lives and to empower people especially the Less Privileged in the rural poor communities. Therefore, the name, 'Cepman' as I now bear is a name of purpose to fulfil a vision-driven destiny that has the 'less privileged' at its centre. What a great yearning!

Also, think of Joseph whose yearning and hope were 'kingly' in dimension. And he nurtured his yearning power with which he eventually ascended on to occupy a kingly position as a preserver of lives. Nobody can stop you from yearning. No force can contain your inner yearning powers, none! You are the only one who can muzzle it.

That lofty aspiration you did once have that you have jettisoned? Did you once have the true and honest yearning to be a leader, an outstanding athlete, or an accomplished professional in a given field? Where is that desire? Remember that "Naked I see the camp of those who desire nothing." I believe that God made every man with a longing to make a difference. That longing which of course is your yearning power is part of your make-up. All you need to do is fan it to flame. Nurture it by dreaming special and BIG to meet a need in life. I know very strongly that there is something special in this life that your heart honestly and earnestly goes out for. That 'something' is a strong indication of your ability to reach out. It doesn't matter if you once failed; you must keep yearning.

I recall the story of *Jim Galvin*; he failed so much in his first business that he had to auction, and he ended up paying for the last battery components with a few hundred dollars he had left. That eventually became what you know today as Motorola. Guess what *Galvin* said after this experience, *"You will know failure, just keep reaching out"*. Now, that's what yearning power is all about. When *Alexandra the Great* was setting out on one of his campaigns, he was distributing numerous gifts to his friends. In his generosity he had given out all his possessions. *"Sir", said one of his friends, "you will have nothing left for yourself." "Oh yes I have", said Alexander, "I still have my hopes".* Now, that's yearning power.

Everything you will ever have or accomplish in this life is carried inside the womb of your yearning capacity. Your yearning power is the engine room of every other thing in life. You must develop and nurture your hopes, dreams and aspirations. You must constantly keep them aflame. Beware of indifference and complacency, for they are the forces that drain you of impetus for accomplishing the impossible and verbalizing same. Take one step at a time towards your yearnings. And when I talk of yearning, I mean big and high expectations that focuses on meeting a need. Low aims are the greatest crime of all. *Marion Jones*' yearning power was so great because she incubated her dreams to be of a king size. She yearned for 5 gold medals at the 2000 Sydney Olympic Games.

She yearned for it, she declared it and she dared it, whereas the Nigerian Government gathered its entire contingent to the games telling them that the nation would be grateful if they could collectively win 7 gold medals. Sad to think that one individual's yearning power was greater, in this case, than the aspirations of an entire nation of over 120 million people. The result: *Marion Jones*, the "big-yearner", Won 5 medals (3 gold & 2 bronze), Nigeria the "low aimer" got not even a gold medal. Greatness answers to its principle and not persons. Yearning is one of such principles. Do you still have your hopes? Is your yearning power kicking? Think about it! (Extracted and paraphrased from a book written by - Kaaka Fegalo).

CHAPTER FOUR

UNDERSTANDING PROSPERITY

What is prosperity?

To define prosperity had often seemed too hard that it has suffered limitation and misconception in the hands of men both in the sense of its definiteness and in the scale or measure of its achievement. Of course, it has always been difficult to arrive at a generally accepted definition of prosperity. Nonetheless, prosperity is the only one achievement in life with the greatest taste. Prosperity is a package for a fulfilled life of greatness that is sealed up in dimensions. A package that man is yet to fully understand and unfold in his life except but only few.

However, *prosperity can be defined as the dimensional blessings of* ***eternal life; sound health; financial wealth; successful marriage; and legacy*** *which together transcends to be the ultimate essence for living as wrapped up in a man's destiny for the purpose of revealing God's glory and to glorify Him.*

Prosperity can also be defined as the dimensional or manifold blessings that brings you into God's abundance life experience of having ***eternal life;*** *living in* ***sound health;*** *owing and possessing* ***financial wealth;*** *enjoying* ***successful marriage; and*** *living for a* ***legacy*** *to fulfill the purpose of* *living in God's glory (John10v10).*

Prosperity is encompassing of all its five dimensions. As a package designed for man by God, prosperity has spiritual dimension; health dimension; financial dimension; marital dimension; and societal impact in dimension. Prosperity is a reserved inheritance packaged for you by God. From the above definition it is evidently clear that financial wealth is one of the dimensions of prosperity. But it requires your conscious efforts and wholesome commitment for you to artfully create financial wealth if you must own and possess it. To become an owner and possessor of financial wealth is not automatic from God but achievable together with God by consciously creating it. It is so experiential that you can actually create financial wealth for yourself and enjoy it right here on earth. Creating, owning and possessing financial wealth is not just an indication of success in life but very much more than that. You can have real taste of the experience of living your life while artfully creating financial wealth.

The abundance life experience that has now been perfected in Christ Jesus was exactly what God had wanted Adam to live in and enjoy in the Garden of Eden. One of such dimensions of the abundance life is to continue to own and possess financial wealth while in the Eden. Unfortunately Adam carelessly lost out this inherited dimension of prosperity, hence man found himself living outside of the Garden in poverty. Not until after many generations had gone. God found, choose and called Abraham with whom He reestablished His covenant for man's restoration to the prosperity of financial wealth which is a dimension of the manifold blessings of God. According to the writer of Psalms, this same covenant that God made with Abraham, He later made to become an Oath to Isaac and a confirmation to Jacob *(Ps.105v8-10)*.

"Now Abraham was old, advanced in age; and the LORD has blessed Abraham in all things (eternal life unto glory; sound health; wealth and riches, successful marriage, and legacy). The LORD has blessed my master greatly (given him prosperity), and he has become great; He has given him flocks and herds, silver and gold, male and female servants, and camels and donkeys" (Gen.24v1, 35).

"Then the LORD appeared to him (Isaac) and said: ..., I will be with you and bless you. The man (Isaac) began to prosper, and continued prospering until he became prosperous" (Gen.26v2-5, 13).

"Thus the man (Jacob) became exceedingly prosperous, and had large flocks, female and male servants, and camels and donkeys. And He blessed him there" (Gen.30v43, 32v29).

To us Christians who now are children and descendants of Abraham through faith, this dimension of God's manifold blessings of the covenant are transferred. Thus, God said to Abraham, I will bless you including your descendants (give you prosperity including that of financial wealth of which you must create your own portion) and you shall be a (a partaker of prosperity) blessing. Certainly Abraham was blessed by God with great financial wealth because he never ceased from creating it. And Abraham with his descendants continued to be abundantly rich. It is quite obvious that financial wealth as a dimension of God's manifold blessings is transferable in every generation but only to those who would care to continue to artfully create it. Obviously, you will have a slim prospect of achieving other dimensions of prosperity while here on earth, if you live in poverty.

The theology of prosperity in connection to creating financial wealth

Creating financial wealth is a great experience that brings great happiness. From the scriptures, there is attested revelation truth that it is actually possible for anyone to experience and enjoy living in the prosperity of financial wealth. Let us explore these scriptures.

"Peace be within your walls, Prosperity within your palaces"- Ps122v7.

Figuratively, while your walls could be your life, your palaces could mean your days of life. And God is simply saying that you would not lack to live in financial wealth within your days of life on earth.

"Now in my prosperity I said, "I shall not be moved"- Ps30v6.

When you find yourself creating, owning and possessing financial wealth, hence you won't be moved by the threatening, dreadful and destructive hands of poverty because you are securely living in financial wealth.

"He himself shall dwell in prosperity, And his descendants shall inherit the earth"- Ps25v13. "And thus you shall say to him who lives in prosperity…" – 1Sam.25v6.

You, in particular shall dwell or live in prosperity – financial wealth by creating it. The possibility of you dwelling or living in financial wealth is certain but only if you make determination to artfully create it. To dwell or live in financial wealth by creating it is to live free from poverty. Then shall you leave behind at least remnant of an inheritance of financial wealth by creating it for your descendants who shall inherit the earth to live on after you are gone.

"…He brings out those who are bound into prosperity…"- Ps.67v6.

Yes, in Christ and through your salvation in Him, God has brought us who believe, out of poverty that we may be bound to financial wealth.

A man is designed and destined to create, own and possess financial wealth. Creating financial wealth makes you to become an inheritor of the goodness of the earth. The prosperity experience of living in financial wealth is so tasty that you can't afford to live on earth and miss it. Friend, you should strive at all cost with every sacrifice it may require from you to create financial wealth in life. When you get yourself out of poverty by creating financial wealth, it brings great pleasure to God. *"...the Lord...Who has pleasure in the prosperity of His servant" (Ps.35v27)*.

Creating financial wealth is an essence for living

The eternal exceedingly great richness of God's financial wealth is earthly transcending in all things and through all things that man may fully partake of it. God being so magnanimous, has destined man to own and possess financial wealth by artfully creating riches while on earth. Hence, God through salvation in His Son made man to become a joint heir with Christ to the prosperity of financial wealth. Of course, you cannot live to enjoy the prosperity of financial wealth if you had failed to artfully create riches to make wealth in your life. It is indeed your sole responsibility to strive to create financial wealth as an essence for your living. To destine you to live in the prosperity of financial wealth is God's own mandate but to artfully create riches to own financial wealth is your own mandate. God had provided you with everything necessary for you to be able to create riches so as to make financial wealth become a reality in your life. The fault and blame is yours not anyone else if you are living in poverty rather than living in riches.

A self-fulfillment need

Every living human is ultimately seeking in life to meet diverse self-fulfillment need. And one of this self-fulfillment need is to own and possess financial wealth. Financial wealth ownership and possession is a dream-need of everyone. One of the great expectations, targets and wishes of every sensible man and woman is to own and possess financial wealth. The need to own and possess financial wealth is one of the complex human needs that aids man's survival, sustenance and fulfillment in life.

Theologically, Apostle Paul did have an understanding of man's complex needs of which financial wealth ownership and possession is one of it when he said, *"and my God shall supply all your need (both your complex need and your basic need (Math.6v25-34) according to His riches (prosperity) in glory by Christ Jesus" (Ph.4v19)*. One of such need that he prayed God to supply was the need for financial wealth. Financial wealth as a dimension of prosperity is an eternal fold of God's blessing that has been made manifest by His mighty power and acts through Christ Jesus. Whatever that the prosperity of financial wealth represents was made manifest in Christ – He is the rich and wealthy king by whose eternal choice of becoming poor, we were made to become rich in financial wealth as He is. God offered

Christ to man to epitomize every dimension of prosperity of which financial wealth as a self-fulfillment need is one of it. So yearn for it and decide to artfully create financial wealth for yourself and become rich in life. You really deserve it.

Devise your plans by which you can create financial wealth

What is plan? And of what form can a plan take? A plan is a calculated step or path to be followed for doing things. It is also a line of action or proposal by which a thing is to be done. It can as well be seen as a wise direction to get something done. Of form, a plan could either be a derived counsel, a thought of an idea in the heart, or a way on how and by which a set goal can be achieved. In setting up your plans, it could be a short term, medium term or long term plans. While short term plans usually runs within weeks to months; medium term plans usually runs within months to say one year; and long term plans usually runs for more than a year. Of course if you are setting a goal for yourself to create financial wealth to be rich, then you must devise financial oriented plans.

The founder of Living Faith Church, David Oyedepo; says, *"Men are in sizes, but life is in phases"*. Relatively I will say that, 'prosperity is in dimensions, but the devised plans to actualize each of its dimensions differs'. By destiny God has played His own part having given you His 'will' and power to create financial wealth but you must play your own part of devising financial oriented plans by which you can get it done. You must personally rise to the responsibility of devising your own unique financial oriented plans by which you would be able to create financial wealth to be rich. Your failure to devise financial oriented plans to create financial wealth is a planning by you to continually live in poverty.

If at your silver age of 25 years, you are yet to have any devised financial oriented plans by which you intend to create financial wealth, then at your golden age of 50 years you shouldn't be surprised if you still found yourself as a helpless prey trapped in the cagy web of chronic poverty. Listen, when you don't make financial oriented plans in life, you make yourself to pay dearly for it. When you don't devise financial oriented plans, never will you decode any future that is full of financial wealth for you.

Obviously there are two kinds of financial oriented plans by which you can succeed in creating financial wealth to be rich in life. The **devised financial oriented plans** and the **revealed financial oriented plans**. Devised financial oriented plans are the personal plans that a man makes by which he seeks and intends to actualize his desired set goal of creating financial wealth to become rich in life. The major source base from which you can devise your personal financial oriented plans include; your human intellect and acquired knowledge; available trending facts and information at your reach; your record of observations; your personal exposure and experience; the history you grew up to know and events you either heard or attend; other people's influence on you; and your personal thought of ideas.

On the other hand, revealed financial plans are the unknown higher financial oriented ways and thoughts of God by which He has designed to take you through in order to enable you to create financial wealth for you to become rich than you never had expected, in accordance with His own 'perfect will' for you. This kind of plans are usually not of human origin but originates expressly from God. The core source base from which a man can receive revealed financial oriented plans is usually through deep thought of ideas either inspired or influenced by your knowledge of God's Word or by express revelation from the Holy Spirit via the channel of human counsel or advice, direction or leading, personal couching or contact, reading books. When you are choked up with your devised financial oriented plans to create your desired financial wealth to be rich, at that point you needed a revealed financial oriented plans. Where the devised financial oriented plans of a man stops working and fails; a revealed financial oriented plans of God begins working from there and succeeds.

Personally in my life I have had cases of where revealed financial oriented plans did prevail over my devised financial oriented plans. After I graduated from the university, one of my immediate devised financial oriented plans was to pursue a master and doctoral degree programs in Economics or International Development at any of the reputable universities in America; after which I had intended to either take up a lecturing career as a professor or work with any of the United Nations Organizations. By this plan I had thought I would be able to create financial wealth to become rich faster, since the plan seemed to be more financially oriented and lucrative.

But behold I never know that God had a better plan that is more financially oriented, which He do rather revealed to me. And that revealed financial oriented plan which I later discovered was better than my originally devised financial oriented plan is to become God's servant called to work in His vineyard as a preacher of the gospel of Jesus Christ, my Lord and Savior. Without delay I quickly abandoned my initially devised financial oriented plan and enrolled for theological training. And here I am today doing kingdom exploits to God's glory, with no sense of regret but with a better fulfillment, considering the level at which God has for years now being helping me to create financial wealth.

Also, when it was time for me to get married, I had my own devised financially oriented plan to marry an already finished and working class woman whom I thought would be more resourceful and financially lucrative; not only to aid me succeed faster in my ministry and possibly make a successful marriage, but also to greatly strengthen my financial foundation to be able to create financial wealth to become rich faster than my colleagues. But at the end, it was God's revealed financial oriented plan that eventually prevailed. And His better revealed financial oriented plan for me was to marry a woman that I would build up by myself from scratch. I am happy I did and grateful to God for His better plan. Why? Because, today I am not only one of the few men on earth that are experiencing and enjoying successful marriage; but also I have learnt through the start-at-the-scratch experience, how to create financial wealth from the scratch out of nothing. And today, the level of financial wealth that God had helped me to create, I really did create it from the scratch out of nothing.

"A man's heart plans his way, but the LORD directs his steps" (Prb.16v9). Of course, it is of your duty to devise and make financial oriented plans of how you could create your desired financial wealth. Your devised or self-made financial oriented plans obviously would become your mapped out steps by which you intend to create your

desired financial wealth to be rich. However, it is of God's to direct the financial oriented plans that you make without which you may not sail or go through with them, especially if He has a better one for you. So even in the midst of making your financial oriented plans, you still need God's hand to direct you aright.

"There are many plans in a man's heart, nevertheless the LORD's counsel – that will stand" (Prb.19v21). Truly, God does have His own designed financial oriented plans that could be revealed to you when your own devised financial oriented plans are not in line with His purpose for your life. You may read these scriptural passages below, they are all an indication to the above fact *(Ps.33v11, 73v24, Ps.25v4, 40v5, 92v5-6, Is.55v8-9).* Yes, you are permitted to devise or make a catalogue of financial oriented plans by which you intend to actualize your life-goal of creating financial wealth to be rich. But sometimes you discover that they may not be working out for you. In that case God obviously has a better and best designed financial oriented plans that He wants to lend to you for a breakthrough in creating financial wealth.

For instance, right from the womb, God had given His 'will' to Jacob the birthright to inherit his father's covenant blessings of financial wealth to be rich *(Rom.9v11-13).* And while still inside the womb, Jacob devised a financial oriented plan to use forceful struggle to make his way out of the womb before his brother Esau, so that he would be declared the first son who shall take over the birthright to inherit the covenant blessings of financial wealth from his father. Unfortunately, the plan that Jacob devised failed to succeed. Perhaps because that was not how God had planned to hand over to him, his father's covenant blessings of financial wealth. Not until his mother Rebekah received a reveal financial oriented plan from God by which Jacob eventually succeeded in taking over from Esau the birthright to inherit his father's covenant blessings of financial wealth. Personal plans made by man to create financial wealth can fail but every revealed plans received from God never fail. Rebekah was sure that the revealed plan she received from God was going to work out perfectly. No wonder without mincing words, she affirmatively spoke to Jacob in confidence saying, *"but his mother said to him, let your curse be on me, my son; only obey my voice, and go, get them for me" (Gen.27v13).*

Am sure after he had the dream to become a leader over his brothers, that Joseph might have started devising maybe little plans on how his dream of becoming a leader could help him to create financial wealth in life. But unknown to his brothers it was their decision to sell Joseph to Egypt that ironically turned out to be God's revealed plan by which his dream later became a reality. And he eventually became a leader and administrator as a prime minister, a position that eventually offered him an opportunity to create financial wealth.

The same case it was with the Israelites while in exile in Egypt. When the suffering and oppression of the Israelites became unbearable for them, I guess that they might have started devising plans on how they could liberate themselves from their poverty stricken living condition. But it was the bold decision of Moses's mother to hide him by the river bank that turned out to be a revealed plan by which God eventually raised Moses to become their great Deliverer and Leader through whom they were victoriously led out of Egypt into the promised land of Canaan where they began to create and possess their own desired financial wealth.

Remember too, that David was a poor shepherd boy wandering in bush, whom am sure might have been devising his own plan on how he can create financial wealth that could accord him social recognition. However, it was his inspired decision to challenge and fight Goliath and his Philistines army that turn out to be a revealed plan from God by which he was eventually made a king and then after he took over the royal throne from King Saul, which actually presented to him great opportunity to create enormous financial wealth.

"Counsel in the heart of man is like deep water, but a man of

understand will draw it out" (Prb.20v5). Not minding your numerous plans on how you can create financial wealth, sometimes you need to draw them out to allow God to give you a revealed plan. Especially when the going has gotten so tough that the plans you have made seem not to be working for you to be able to create your desired financial wealth.

"A man's steps are of the LORD, how then can man understand his own way?" (Prb.20v24). The above scripture is simply implying that when you completely seem not to know which financial oriented plan (way) to devise, by which you can create your desired financial wealth, you absolutely at such moment needed to depend on God to receive a revealed steps (plans) from Him *(Deut.29v29, Ps.25v14, Amos3v7).* As you depend on God for a better revealed plan, it will be best if you begin now to roll out your own devised plan on how to create financial wealth. With a well devised plan you will navigate over your problems without excusing yourself from becoming an owner and possessor of financial wealth.

CHAPTER FIVE

NO EXCUSES FOR BEING POOR IN LIFE

Never lock yourself up with your problems

Never should you dare to take the risk of locking yourself up with the padlock of your problems. Else if you do, then it will be too difficult for you to create financial wealth. Man has always made his problems to become the strongest padlock with which he has continued to lock himself into poverty. Understand that it is your sole choice either or not to unlock financial wealth into your life. Listen, men who choose to lock themselves up with their problems do always accuse their problems for their failure to become rich in life. Your greatest chance to unlock open financial wealth would only begin when you stop pointing an accusing finger on your own problems. You must cease from putting your problems up as excuses. Otherwise if you continue to do so, it won't be long you might begin to face the combine battles of mediocrity, failure and frustration, poverty and loss of hope for a better future.

Arrest your problems, don't accuse them

Men who will tomorrow obviously create and live to enjoy financial wealth as a dimension of prosperity are those who would take bold steps today to arrest their problems. And not those who accuse their problems. Someone says, *"the most unprofitable item ever manufactured is an excuse"*. To create financial wealth requires that you step out bold to arrest your problems, and not to accuse them. You become afraid and fearful of your problems once you begin to accuse them and put them up as excuses. But men who are concerned with their problems do live to solve them. While those who worry over their problems do live to be defeated by them.

The problem you fear today may overwhelm you tomorrow. The greatest problem of man is not his problems but the problem of not solving his problems. Man has always accused his problems and used them as excuses for not being able to achieve his set goals in life, especially that of the prosperity of financial wealth. When a man fails to be successful, fails to make great achievements, fails to create financial wealth in life, he would have his problems to accuse and to be his excuses.

"Some men have thousands of reasons why they cannot do what they want to do, when all they need is one reason why they can"- *Willis Whitney*. Simply, ask someone why are you poor and still living with low financial ability. Such one would always have certain problems to accuse as excuses – you see, I am from a poor family; I don't have a job yet; my current job is not befitting; my income is too small; my business is not

doing well; I am not a graduate; I can't access huge initial take off capital; I have nobody to help me out with a better stuff out there; I am duped or robbed my life savings or huge amount of money; there is an evil power working against me, etc.

But hear this, if Zacchaeus could climb the Sycamore tree, your height shouldn't be an excuse. If David could kill Goliath at the age of 17 years, your age as a young person shouldn't be an excuse. If Joseph as a slave could become a Prime minister in Egypt, alien status as a migrant shouldn't be an excuse. If the woman with the issue of blood could stretch at her last strength to touch the helm of Jesus' garment, your indisposed condition shouldn't be an excuse. If the poor widow could give out her last penny as offerings, your poverty state shouldn't be an excuse. If Daniel could fearlessly meet with the lions, being afraid of anything, not even death should be an excuse for you. *"Only you and you alone can change your situation. Don't blame it on anything or anyone" – Leonardo Dicaprio.* No more excuses. Get inspired and move on. Stop making excuses. Stop procrastinating. Do the needful now not now after.

Before now I was once also thinking that I had a lot of problems for which reason I won't be able to achieve the prosperity of financial wealth. In those days of my past I discovered that I too was not having most of these things mentioned above. I felt then that my problems were insurmountable that I cannot solve them. Back then I accused my own problems as excuses. Perhaps, this is your own case now. The good news is that even with your problems, you can still achieve your own prosperity of financial wealth. However, even if all the problems mentioned earlier seem to be your problems too, there are still solutions to them. Though they might be quite challenging, yet you should not take them as a justification to disqualify yourself from being a candidate of financial wealth. *"To surrender to opposition is to lose your position"- David Oyedepo.*

No matter what your problems may be; never you make excuses with your problems but make execution of your plans to overcome your problems. You don't have to salute your problems but solve your problems. Don't ever pretend over your problems but prevail over your problems. You can't afford to be a prey to your problems but be a predator to your problems. You must not allow your problems to limit you but you should look for a way to liberate yourself from your problems. Don't give up and don't surrender to your problems but give all to subdue your problems. There is always a solution to every problem in life. Stop discovering why you can't solve your problems, but rather discover how you can solve your problems. Don't think they are enough to stop you from achieving your set goal in life. Only you can stop yourself not your problems.

I only dare men but I don't stop men

All men are equal but not all men are able. Every man is born to meet problems and to solve problems. Men who took a dogged stand to solve their problems have in every ages created and sustained for themselves a lasting treasure of financial wealth that have given their personality a great influence and power. They refused neither to quit nor surrender to Mr. Problems of life. Today they are fulfilled men of greatness, standing taller at various corners of the world in the midst of many other men of failures. All because they have been able to secure a solution warrant with which they did arrest their problems and conquered all odds. *"Begin while others make excuses. Keep going while others are quitting"* – *Billy Cox*. Below is the testimony of some successful great men who despite their big problems had created financial wealth and are now living to enjoy it.

"I struggled academically throughout elementary school yet I became the best Neurosurgeon in the world in 1987" – *Dr. Ben Carson*.

"I was rapped at the age of 9 yet I am one of the most influential women in the world" – *Oprah Winfrey*.

"I didn't even complete my university education but I became the world's richest man" – *Bill Gates*.

"I was sexually, mentally, emotionally and verbally abused by my father as far back as I can remember, until I left home at the age of eighteen, yet I am one of the most influential preachers in the world" – *Joyce Meyer.*

"I told my father that we would be very rich but he couldn't believe me. I made it a reality" – *Christiano Ronaldo.*

"I used to serve tea at a shop to support my football training and still became one of the world's best footballers" – *Lionel Messi.*

"I used to sleep on the floor in my friends' rooms, returning coke bottles for food, money, and getting weekly free meals at a local temple, I later on founded Apple Company" – *Steve Jobs.*

"My teachers used to call me a failure, but I became a Prime Minister" – *former British Prime Minister, Tony Blair.*

"I started living faith church (aka. Winners Chapel) from a lawn tennis court with three members only and preach prosperity. Many of my friends criticized me, but today we have the largest church auditorium in the world and two world-class universities" – *Bishop David Oyedepo.*

"I was in prison for 27years and still became president of my country, South Africa" – *Nelson Mandela.*

"I drove a taxi to finance my university education but today I am a billionaire" – *Mike Adenuga (CEO, Globacom, a telecommunication giant in Nigeria).*

"I was on the verge of suicide when an idea of opening a restaurant hit me after I retired as a cook in the navy" – *Harland Sanders, Founder of KFC.*

"I worked for my uncle since I was a small boy, people looked down on me. I later on took a loan from my uncle open a tiny shop, I worked hard to make ends meet. Now I am the world's richest man in Africa" – *Aliko Dangote.*

"I am a son of a black immigrant from Kenya, I graduated from Harvard and later on became a senator in Chicago. Now I am the president of the most powerful nation on earth" – *Barak Hussein Obama.*

"I travel to America in search of financial independence when I was 15years old. I became the world's most-strongest man 7 times and once won the Mr. Universe. I then got my economics degree, then I became one of Hollywood's best actors before I was voted twice as governor of California, the world's richest state after France and Britain" – *Arnold Swarzzenegger.*

With a strong self-will a man arrests his life-never ending problems with a handcuff of solution, one at a time just as they appear before him. A strong self-will that is backed up with positive mindset is all that you need to surmount your problems no matter how tough they might appear. Someone says, *"97% of people who quit too soon are employed by the 3% who never give up". "The situation you don't address you cannot arrest"- David Abioye.* Men who are fulfilling their destiny in the area of creating financial wealth and, who today are living to enjoy riches have before now risen up to arrest their own (Mr.) problems of life which had once stood against them. And under their arrest custody, Mr. Problems of life has itself made this following confessional statement. Hear out its touching confession!

"I am Mr. Problems of life. I originated from the time of man's origin. So, I am as old as man. I both live and exist with every man. I do stand like mountain, but I can still be leveled down. I do appear like a valley, but I can still be leveled up. I do prove a crooked and rough road to trade on, but I can still be straightened. I do look like a giant but I am not. I am only but the one that challenges men to think creatively. I only dare men but I don't stop men who solve me. Anytime I am solved by men, at that point I am arrested. Though in the hands of time I do regain my freedom and still once again resurface to dare men. This I do because I like being solved by men. You never can arrest me if you choose to run away from me. The only way you can arrest me is to solve me. I am solvable if you care to know. Men with great determination and faith have more than once solved me at different stages in their lives, and I did not stop them.

With my presence, men are challenged to make use of their mind and brain to come up with possibility ideas of solution that could better their lives and their world. This is my unnoticed and unappreciated importance to human existence. My posture is the brain behind the significant breakthroughs that man has ever lived to celebrate in the human history.

What men are living to enjoy today is the outcome of the goals of greatness achieved by men who had taken bold steps to arrest me. Men can accuse me for their failures. Men may even hate me more. Men may still condemn me and crucify me. Perhaps just one day, those men whom I have challenged to achieve a fulfilled life of greatness will discharge and acquit me from all accusations leveled against me by men who do fail to solve me. Who knows! Remember, I only dare men but I don't stop men".

What an inspiring philosophical wise saying. Nothing else than this wise saying has said it all and painted the most crystal picture of the problems of life. We could notice its origin, meaning, nature and essence. Problems are part of life and one is sure to face them in life. In fact, no one is exempted from its certainties.

Robert Schuller has this to say about problems, "the point is clear: Nobody is free from problems. A problem-free life is an illusion-a mirage in the desert. It is a dangerously deception, which can mislead, blind, and distract. To pursue a problem-free life is to run after an elusive fantasy; it is a waste of mental and physical energies. Every living human person has problems". Problems are never overpowering hindrances or obstacles but overcome-able challenges. Decide that you will be successful and happy, come what may; and good things will find you. The roadblocks are only minor obstacles along the way.

"Problems are guide posts not stop posts"- David Oyedepo. They only come to make us stronger and better than we are. Problems are what challenge us to rise up and say, I have got to prove a point that I am made of some great stuff to achieve a great feat in life. Problems cannot stop us from achieving the prosperity of financial wealth in life but our choice not to solve them could be our limitations. Yes, problems can slow the pace of your process to achieve your vision of creating financial wealth; but quitting won't speed up the process either. It matters what you say and do in the face of problems. Never say, I can't solve the problems. And do never surrender nor quit when faced with problems. Challenges makes life interesting; overcoming them makes life meaningful. For a path without obstacles leads nowhere. Of course if you don't climb the mountain; you can't view the plain.

Your mountain sized problems

Yes, problems do stand and appear as mountain, yet you always find a way of either leveling it down or at least climbing on top of it. It is when you have leveled or climbed on top of your mountain sized problems that you will be sure of positive possibilities in life. The gap that separates you from achieving the prosperity of financial wealth is the elevation distance between you and your mountain sized problems. Of course climbing or leveling your mountain sized problems may never be instant but steadily gradual. It therefore takes coming up with solution ideas to gradually but steadily level down or climb atop of your mountain of problems.

Elijah the prophet was a man of God who once in his life time had to face a mountain-sized problem of how he could overcome and totally defeat the terrorizing prophets of Baal and prophetess of Asherah. Eventually he came up with a great solution idea, when he said, *"...then you call on the name of your gods and I will call on the name of the Lord..."* – *(1Kg.18v24)*. With this Elijah's solution idea, not only that he finally defeated them he also executed them all with none unable to escape *(1Kg.18v40)*.

From the level ground where you are today standing and accusing your problems, decide instead to solve them. You can really take off by using your brain to creatively think out some solution ideas that can possibly get your problems solved. Your brain is one of your creative gifted talents that have the richest potential to help you solve your problems. Many today are poor, not because they could not create financial wealth but because they failed to make good use of their brain.

The capacity and potential of our brain has always been under-utilized by many. Man has always been guilty of making a full waste of his brain. No matter the mountain size of your problems, with your faith in God, your brain can do the rest magic to bring it down leveled. Through your subconscious, your creative thinking activates the brain cells that generate possible solution ideas capable of solving your problems. Just begin with the steps of creative thinking and the right ideas will surely come for you to solve your problems. But guess what! If you don't begin here today with steps of creative thinking in your brain, you can't tomorrow get there never without it. Begin with the steps of creative thinking in your brain for solution ideas that can take you off the ground where you are standing to accuse your problems.

Your mind of course is like a gully valley always waiting to be filled up with the creative ideas of solution generated from the brain. The more your brain creatively thinks, the more your mind is filled up with possible solution ideas to solve your problems. Once your mind is filled up with possible solution ideas, you become motivated in your conscious and begin to solve your problems. You become thrilled with positive attitude that propels you to make positive efforts and take right actions toward solving your problems. And before you could know it your problems are solved.

I too have had a lot of problems in life, but God had always helped me to creatively come up with workable solution of ideas which I do make positive effort to apply with the right actions that would be required to solve them. And before you could know it, I would get my problem solved. This has always worked for me.

Nothing happens until something happens. Faith in God plus creative or positive thinking for ideas are equal to possibility. Solution ideas with right actions and positive efforts give you strength of possibility to solve your problems. With this strength of possibility at your disposal, God complements it with His grace to enable you solve your problems. Otherwise hear what *Robert Schuller* said, *"You won't win, if you don't begin".* You obviously have no reason for you not to create financial wealth. No one has traveled the road of success, without crossing the streets of problems and challenges. God never promised us an easy journey, He only promised us a great destination.

Develop an effective problem solving approach

As a problem solving approach, you just have to accept the fact that everyone has got some problems to face just like you too. Remember, successful people have two things on their lips, "Smile and Silence". Smile can solve problems, while silence can avoid problems. Talking about your problems can become your greatest addiction. Do break the habit. Talk about your joys even in the face of your problems. Don't pray for an easy life; pray for the strength to endure a difficult one. For without the struggles, you will never know your strengths.

However, for any problem you are already facing, always believe that every problem is got to end up one day. *"Nothing is permanent in this world, not even our troubles" - Charlie Chaplin.* Time heals everything. However good or bad a situation is, it will eventually change as times passes on.

Don't rule out that your problems can turn out to bring good to you. Choose to put up a positive attitude and response towards your problems. Take up the positive reactions and solution to solve your problems that would protect the dignity of your person and bring goodness of joy to the people around you. Never with pride look down on your problems else they may bring you into the place hopelessly. Don't ever procrastinate to solving your problems.

Don't allow yourself to add to your problems by apportioning blames or faulting someone out there. Try to understand what exactly is your problem so as to avoid a mix up and you end up missing out the axe head. Come up with an incentive decisions and actions to seize opportunities to solve your problems.

With creative thinking electrify your brain with your problems so as to enable it breed up into your mind some possible solution ideas that could solve them. With a committed interest, channel all resources within your disposal toward solving your problems. Reach out to people to involve them in solving your problems. Don't be equally yoked with possibility unbelievers or share in their ideas. Persist day in-day out until you solve your problems.

Until you endeavor to sell out some brain-manufactured ideas of solution to your problems, you will never get any impressive turnover record of solving them. Should you allow this mental-business situation to happen in your life, then never will you make any geometric profit of solution to solve your problems. Never dare to run away from your problems. *"Tough times never last but tough people do"*- Robert Schuller.

Always pluck out some seed of possible solution ideas from the tree of your brain into your mind to solve your problems. Otherwise your problems will pluck you away from the tree of achieving the prosperity of financial wealth that you desire. Don't elude yourself the chance of achieving greatness in life just because you have couple of problems that seem unsolvable to you. Just develop the above problem solving approaches and it won't be long you will have solved your problems. Know that no matter how bad things seem to be, they will always get better. The hardest winter always follows the warmth of spring.

All you need do is to always approach your problems like an Eagle especially when it faces a windy storm. Instead of seeing a windy storm as a problem, Eagles rather love the windy storms: When clouds gather, the eagle gets excited; the eagle uses the windy storm to lift itself higher. Once it finds the stormy wind, the eagle locks its wings to brace the storm to lift itself above the clouds. This gives the eagle an opportunity to glide and rest its wings. In the meantime, all the other birds hide in branches and leaves of the tree. That is to say, challenges will come your way as long as you live on earth. Face your challenges head on; knowing that these will make you emerge stronger and better than you were. We can use the storms of life to rise to greater heights. Achievers are not afraid of storms they find a way of adapting to the new challenges to rise to greater heights. Achievers are not afraid of challenges; they are 'solutionists' to challenges and problems. They relish the challenges and use them profitably. Do away with fear, for you can do it.

CHAPTER SIX

RESOURCES FOR CREATING FINANCIAL WEALTH

You need God and His grace:

"Then you say in your heart, my power and the might of my hand have gained me this wealth (of prosperity). And you shall remember the LORD your God, for it is He who gives you power to get (create) wealth (of prosperity)...". God is the greatest amongst the fundamental resources that you will need to be able to create financial wealth as a dimension of prosperity. Without God, your chances to be a beneficial partaker in the prosperity of financial wealth may totally collapse down. *Hear what Martin Luther says, "God created the world out of nothing and as long as we are nothing, He can make something out of us".* And I say, not only out of us but even for us.

You obviously need to place God ahead of you in all your plans and efforts to create financial wealth. Always plan with God ahead and be proactive in your planning. He that plans the future with God, works less in the future. When you do plan with God, He grants you His divine grace for uncommon speed ahead of others in achieving a fulfilled life of greatness. Without God in your life who alone is able to do exceeding great things, you won't be able to do and achieve even the smallest and least things in life. You actually need God, He who made all visible things from the invisible things to make the prosperity experience of financial wealth a visible reality in your life. Indeed, you need He who calls things that do not exist yet as though they are in existence to call up the fullest of financial wealth into your life.

And how can you actually get God involved in your life as a resource for creating financial wealth? It is simply by having absolute faith in God. For without faith you cannot please God to help you out to overcome whatever may be standing on your way *(Heb.11v6)*. Faith in God enables you not to be troubled or worried of seeming problems and challenges no matter how enormous they may appear. Worry, anxiety and fear, all are always an absence of faith. *According to John Mason, "worry is the triumph of fear over faith; A route that leads from somewhere to nowhere".* In fact, without faith in God you will be deterred to get to nowhere closer to creating financial wealth. *A Swedish proverb says, "Worry gives a small thing a big shadow".* But I tell you what! Faith in God sees every big problems or challenges as a small shadow that will soon disappear. *"For all I have seen teaches me to trust the creator for all I have not seen" – Emerson Waldo.*

It is an absolute faith in God that will give birth in you the confidence and the energy that you will require to really create financial wealth. Maybe you are already been knocked down on the ground of lingering unbelief and doubt on whether you can ever become rich. An absolute faith in God could be likened to what *Ramona Carol* said, *"Faith is putting all your eggs in God's basket, then counting your blessings before they hatch"*. An absolute faith in God is one that conquers doubt, fear and unbelief; one that believes without wavering; that sees afar through the eyes of hope; that is alive in its required works etc.

When faith is expressed and backed up with a decision for complete dependence on God, grace becomes activated and active in one's life. You need this grace to receive it from God as favor. And why do you need God's grace by the way? *Because grace is the undeserved help from God that has the divine capacity beyond human strength to enable any man on whom it rests upon to do unusual things and achieve uncommon things for a great experience in life. In other words, grace can as well be referred as the unmerited favor of the divine help that God gives to a man to enable him beyond his self-effort and strength to do or achieve a great thing in life.* Of course, achieving the prosperity of financial wealth in life is a great feat. And you definitely do need God's grace.

No matter how far you may think that your self-effort and strength could take you, still you should solely depend on God's grace. If not, your strength and self-effort alone may disappoint you or end up being in vain. When you are making effort without grace to create financial wealth in order to live to enjoy riches, it may become an attempt in futility. But with grace you are sure of hitting it big to be rich without disgrace. This much needed grace, God would always power upon you through His Spirit. The grace of God provides you with an unusual ability and strength to do extra-ordinary exploits in life. For it is not of he who wills nor of he who runs to be rich, but it is of God who gives grace to become rich. Am pretty sure He wants you to be rich. Without grace you become bound naked with your effort and strength without meaningful results.

Therefore, you must acknowledge the grace of God so much so that you should seek for it and depend on God for it. If at all you want to create financial wealth to enjoy riches in life. Only then will you see God amplify and magnify your effort and strength for you to be able to achieve the prosperity of financial wealth.

You need Network of people

Without money you may struggle to become rich in life. But without people you may never discover where and how to make money. In the journey to creating financial wealth, you will not get to anywhere without someone giving you a lifting hand somewhere. Without people reaching out their helping hands to you, to achieve the prosperity of financial wealth in life, it may turn out to become a mission impossible. No man anywhere is an island. And even an island is in need of a man for it to be discovered, explored and or inhabited. Just as an Island, you too need someone. Without God using people to help you climb up the lather of creating financial wealth, you will not by chance in life get anywhere near to it.

The more people you can influence, the more successful you will be in life. Develop the attitude of connecting with people. Anywhere you go to, learn to appreciate people. Be people oriented and be people friendly. You should wisely build up a network of right people around you who are to serve as your human resource base of whom you can always call or depend on, either now or latter. People from whom you would also be receiving right encouragement, support, knowledge and advice capable of helping you in your effort and bidding to create financial wealth. You need people who will always stand by you, especially when the going seems tough.

Sugar and salt may be mixed together but ants rejects the salt and carry only the sugar. Select the right people in life that could make your life better and more successful. People who would encourage you even in your discouraging situations of life; these people keep you going with encouraging words. People whose hands are stronger enough to hold yours up; to give you a lifting especially when you are weak and down. People who would mention your name and advertise you in the quarters where your skills and talents are needed for a reward. Build a network of people and identify yourself with associations that will serve as leverages for opportunities and connections.

No man anywhere has become or achieved anything without someone else. Whatever you will become or achieve in life, you will not become or achieve it without other people. You really need network of certain right people in your life that will stand as human resource catalyst to enable you either as a way of help or as a matter of obligation to ensure that you succeed becoming a rich man or woman. As a resource base I too have such network of wonderful people through whom God have continued to help me get to where I am now. When you fail to build up for yourself this network of human resource base, you would sooner or later found yourself in the ditch of unreachable distance, mistakes, discouragement, loneliness, complaining, denial and failure. Next you may find yourself become an accuser of brethren, accusing and blaming this or that person for not doing this or that to help you to create financial wealth.

Of course, as you build up a network of people, you should equally not only make a mastery of but build up good human relation principles and goodwill toward the same people. Value those people, friends and family members who have supported and encouraged you and be there for them as well. With a good human relation approach, you will be able to relate with the people smoothly, influence them to your advantage and eventually win their support towards helping you to make an art craft of creating your own financial wealth afterward. Building a network of right people around you who could be a catalyst to you will help you to ensure continuity in your pursuance to creating financial wealth, which at all does not deserve quitting. People who would be honest enough to caution you when you are wrong; they prevent you from digging a grave mistake that may bury your destiny dimension of create financial wealth.

Nevertheless, *Mark Twain says, "keep away from people who try to belittle your ambitions. Small people always do that, but the really great people make you feel that you too can become great".* In other words, not everybody will be meant by God to be an angelic helper to you on your way to creating financial wealth. Never should you think so. In fact, while certain people will definitely be as such to you, certain others will definitely be enemies to hinder you from creating financial wealth in life. In this world, people will always throw stones on the path of your success. But it depends on what you make from them – either a wall, then you will be stocked in at your base level or a bridge then you will crossover to the next level.

In reality, sometimes you actually need such people who may appear to be enemies to you. Ironically they may be the people that could indirectly become so instrumental in aiding you to create financial wealth. Sometimes for you to succeed in life you need enemies…Yes!!! You need people who will mock you, so that you can run to God. You need people who will try to intimidate you, so that you can be courageous. You need people who will say 'No' so that you can learn how to be independent…I mean how to do it yourself. You need people who will disappoint you so that you can believe in yourself. You need people who will sell your Joseph so that you can get to your Egypt and become a prime minister in a strange land of destiny.

You need Prayer

No Christian anywhere who succeeds with a drought and famine stricken prayer-lifestyle. Prayer is a strategic resource required for daily sustenance of victory over opposition to greatness and for survival to future greatness in life. Without prayer you may find yourself in life struggling and stumbling instead of progressively creating financial wealth. Through prayer you invite God into the affairs of your life to direct, lead, guide and enable you not only to succeed in doing extraordinary exploits but also to achieve the prosperity of financial wealth as a great feat. Through prayer you challenge every destiny attackers; frustrate every destiny falters; overcome every destiny obstructers; defeats every destiny destroyers; pray through your destiny from the hands of evil forces and powers.

According to *Mark Littleton*, *"through prayer you turn your doubts to questions, turn your questions to prayers and turn your prayers to God. The greatest tragedy of life is not unanswered prayer, but unoffered prayer"* – F. B. Meyer. Meanwhile according to O. Hallesby, *"mind you that prayer is not a gadget we use when nothing else works, but even when everything is working"*. Constantly and consistently offer prayers to God to clear and smoothen your way for you to be able to create financial wealth at ease and then enjoy it in life.

You need Money

Without money you cannot pay your way through to the destination of creating financial wealth. Yes, it is just as simple as that. While here on earth, you either need to borrow money or earn money to be able to achieve the prosperity of financial wealth. Of course to steal is not an option. There was a story of a pastor who on the ground of building a mega ministry abroad defrauded unsuspecting victims of huge amount of money which he claimed after he was arrested by the police that he sowed out the same money as spiritual seed to other bigger ministries with the hope that God would prosper and make him rich in ministry. That is purely an error.

It is rather far better for you to earn money than to borrow money to become rich. Let alone stealing, for stealing is the worst that carries along it a curse. The prosperity experience of owning, possession and enjoying financial wealth is a life time project, so you can't depend on borrowing all through your life time to finance its achievement. With this option, you stand the risk of going bankrupt which can for life liquidate your opportunity to ever create financial wealth. It is obviously better for you to begin to do something to earn money in order to finance your effort to create financial wealth. No matter how little is that thing you may be doing, provided it is something good that one should be doing. And no matter the smallest of penny you begin to earn at inception. For according the wise saying of Solomon, *"a living dog is better than a dead lion"*. Meaning that he who does the least of a menial job is far better than he who is idle. And of course, he who earns a penny is better off than he who earns nothing.

You need Info-Knowledge and Wisdom:

Knowledge can be acquired but common sense which is natural wisdom is an inbuilt higher knowledge. If you must succeed in creating financial wealth, you need to develop and apply your natural wisdom or sense. Education and natural sense are never the same. Yes, by education you acquire knowledge. Yet, it is a million times better to have natural wisdom or sense than to have education without it. No wonder, men with natural wisdom who dropped out of school without proper education even became millionaires.

Education which produces knowledge is light while natural wisdom or sense which is higher inbuilt knowledge is the switch to turn it on. Light is never on until you switch it on.

Your knowledge is your greatest investment in life. A man without information is like the dead in the grave. And without knowledge you will stink into the ditch of ignorance. While knowledge is the highest level of information, yet information brings knowledge. This kind of knowledge that information brings is what I call, "info-knowledge".

Commit yourself to sourcing information and acquiring knowledge through such learning processes as - reading, listening, watching, observation or studying so as to upgrade your level of info-knowledge. Without you having this info-knowledge, you will only make less impact or have little chance to create financial wealth. I guess it was this info-knowledge that God meant when He says, *"my people perish for lack of knowledge" (Hos.4v6)*. Go for it now. The writer of proverb says; a wise man is strong, yes a man of knowledge increases in strength, of course to do more exploit in life than others *(Prb.24v4-5)*.

Now why do you even need info-knowledge as a resource for creating financial wealth? It is because 'Knowledge' is not just money but time and power. But perhaps you don't know that time is money and power. You must embark on knowledge acquiring and learning process for you to be better informed. The atmosphere of knowledge is the arena of power. Learning process gives you knowledge which is the highest level of information. And Information on the other hand gives you knowledge. Info-knowledge is the wisdom that edges out challenges. Info-knowledge is what prepares a man ahead of critical times. It is info-knowledge that gives you the strength to stand out a great achiever in the face of challenges. With info-knowledge you can't fail in times of challenging situations. Info-knowledge assures you prospect and gives you hope. Even when you fall, the strength of your info-knowledge gets you up once again.

What you don't have information about, you won't have knowledge of it. And on that you will lack adequate wisdom to take right decisions. Give yourself to a learning process to acquire info-knowledge about wealth creation and the right principles and strategies that could be applied. By so doing you will know the challenges you will face, sacrifices to make and generally what it will take you especially to create your desired financial wealth. *"Great info-knowledge can lead you to dig a well before you are thirsty and plant a seed before you are hungry"- John Mason.* Without info-knowledge one becomes blind to mistakes. It is said that when you are not informed you become deformed. But when you are informed, you become transformed. We are in a highly competitive world full of people who are competing to create a lasting financial wealth for greatness in life.

It is only those who are better off with higher level of info-knowledge acquired through learning process that will eventually prevail despite all odds. It is the quality of the info-knowledge at your disposal that determines the quality of your performance and achievement in life. Info-knowledge provides a man with strategic advantage that enables him to always compete better than others. *"Chance favors the prepared mind"- Louis Pasteur.* Through info-knowledge you will get to know most things that will turn out to become useful and helpful in helping you to create financial wealth. Such info-knowledge now or latter will help you to attend and resolve most hypothetical questions which often may concern your choice to creating financial wealth; such as Why am I poor?, What can I do to be rich?, When do I need to be rich?, How possible is it for me to become rich?, Who do I need that could help me to become rich?, Which opportunities are existing for me to become rich?, and where are these opportunities?. Sometimes these hypothetical questions become intrinsic and or incidental for you to be able to actually create financial wealth.

In your pursuit to achieve the prosperity of financial

wealth, info-knowledge prepares you as a champion ahead of possible challenges. Of course you should know that champions are not made on the day of victory but on the days of preparation. The day of victory only becomes for them the day of celebrating their past days of preparation. A warrior never prepares on the day of war but quite long ahead of it, otherwise he might shamefully be defeated at the war front. Therefore, you must through info-knowledge prepare yourself ahead of the life battle of overcoming challenges and competitions in order to create financial wealth.

You need Action-steps of hard-work

An action-step of hard work produces positive outcomes and results. An action-step of hard work is a fertile ground for creating financial wealth. Symbolically, Jesus spoke about this when He says, *"Most assuredly, I say to you, unless a grain of wheat falls into the ground and dies, it remains alone; but if it dies, it produces much grain"* (John12v24). An action-step of hard work that you take towards creating financial wealth is like a good seed that dies and afterwards germinates to bring forth much fruits of results. Until you take actions of hard work, there would be no result of possibility for you to actually create financial wealth.

Also, in *Jer.4v3*, God spoke to the people of Judah and Jerusalem saying, *"break up your fallow ground, and do not sow among thorns"*. When you begin to take action-steps of hard work in life, it won't be long you would break your fallow ground of poverty with wealth creation. But when you are seeking to create financial wealth without action-steps of hard work, you would fatally be chocked up with thorns of failure.

Isaac, one of the patriarchs, under the scourge of a poverty-stricken famine was forced out of Canaan to wander into the idolatrous nation of Philistine, just in search for a greener pasture. Just right there in a foreign land he took action-steps of hard work by which he was able to break for himself the fallow ground of the prevalent famine and created financial wealth which made him prospered so much that he became so prosperous in riches of material possessions, even to the envy of the Philistines *(Gen.26v12)*.

When God sees your commitment in sowing your seed of action-steps of hard work, He would water it through His divine irrigation mechanism of rewarding with a results. And before you could know it, your actions of hard work as seed will germinate to bring forth positive results and impact in your effort to create financial wealth. If Isaac through the action-step of his hard work was able to achieve his vision of creating financial wealth as a dimension of prosperity, why can't you too. Just work hard every day to be the best person you aspire to be, but never feel guilty if you fall short of your goals. Every sunrise offers a second chance. Don't give up with your action-steps of hard work. It won't be long you will have created your own financial wealth.

You need Strategic Principles

Living your life without principles is like living without discipline. Principles are conceptualized proven ideas that produce results of achievement when applied with strategic and rightfully calculated actions. You need to apply certain business, investment, wealth creation and financial principles with certain strategic action-steps that would effectively enable you to create your desired financial wealth. Therefore, without you applying certain principles with strategic action-steps to utilize emerging opportunities, you may continue to struggle in your effort to create financial wealth. When you create financial wealth it accords you the right and opportunity to control power, command influence, and enjoy fame with honor before men.

ANTHONY CEPMAN A. O.

CHAPTER SEVEN

POVERTY IS A CHOICE NOT BY FATE

Who is a poor man?

Poverty is the act of being poor. And to be poor is a state of financial lack that makes a man unable to afford the basic needs of life namely food, shelter, clothing, and comfort facilities required for daily survival, sustenance and happy living. Therefore, a poor man is not he who lacks money to live in luxury, to acquire material assets and property and or own an income generating business or investments; but a poor man is actually he who lacks money in his pocket to provide himself and or family with the basic provisions of life as named above.

Man made his choice to be poor

The issue of 'why poverty' has always been a great burden to me. To this regard, there are several questions as mentioned below that I have before now continued to ask myself, which for so long a time I have not been able to answer not until recently. Why poverty in the first place? And why are some people poor? Is poverty a phenomenon of creation that originated from God? Does God create some people to be poor and others to be rich? Being poor is it by fate or a choice? To my utmost amazement, I discovered that to be poor in life is a choice. Unfortunately, it was Adam on behalf of the entire human race that made the ugly choice to be poor. To be poor in life or to live in poverty wasn't God's original will for man. It is rather regrettable that quite a great number of people today including many Christians are still taking after the first Adam to make the same choice to be poor in life. Anyway that's your choice! But for me down to my generations unborn I have made a choice to be rich in life.

"The LORD God planted a garden eastward in Eden, and there He put man whom He had formed" (Gen.2v8). I would like you to imagine how rich the Garden of Eden was. Perhaps you don't know that the Garden of Eden is the greatest empire of financial wealth with great possession of riches that has ever been located anywhere on the planet earth since the existence of mankind. Even in the entire years to come there can never be any other empire of financial wealth with such a possession of riches better than Garden of Eden, that anyone else can ever create, own or possess in life. Because it is God's will for man to be financially wealthy and live to enjoy riches, God had to put Adam inside the greatest empire of financial wealth with greatest possession of riches which He had planted and called the Eden Garden.

Adam found himself living as a man who owned, possessed and controlled an uncommon and great financial wealth that was in Eden not until he succumbed to the lies and deception of Satan and made his choice to disobey God which was accounted by God as sin against him. By his choice to disobey God, he consequently made his choice to become poor. And because God respects man's choice, He immediately put Adam off away from the Garden of Eden where he was previously living and enjoying great financial wealth as possessions of an inheritance from the everlasting God who alone is exceedingly rich in financial wealth *(Gen.3v23-24)*. In the world outside the Garden of Eden, Adam still maintained and lived on with his choice to be poor by allowing himself to remain in bondage to the lies and deceptions of Satan. And this Satan's lies and deception to which he was in bondage has the ability to influence every man of Adam's descendant born of a woman to make the same choice of becoming poor in life. The only thing that can break this bondage off your life is God's power. That's the power that comes from God through your knowledge of Him in Christ by wisdom and revelation *(Eph.1v17-19)*.

"And you shall remember the LORD your God, for it is He who gives you power to make (create) wealth, that He may establish His covenant which He swore to your fathers, as it is this day" *(Deut.8v18)*. Through the patriarchs of faith, Abraham, Isaac and Jacob God reestablished His covenant of obedience in order to restore man back to the same

financial wealth that Adam had lost by his choice to disobey God. Then Moses the servant of God reminded the descendants of the patriarchs that God had sworn to bring them into an inheritance of covenant financial wealth which requires the power of God for them to be able to create and enjoy same. For it could only take the power of God for the Israelites to break off their lives from bondage to Satan's lies and deception which could influence them to make the same choice of becoming poor.

If God does not want every man to own and possess financial wealth, then of what need would it be for Him to give power to men to make financial wealth. According to Moses, God is not selective to give His power only to certain people whom alone deserves to create financial wealth. No! Rather, God is He who gives 'you' – inclusive of all the Israelites, even you too, power to create financial wealth. It takes God whose will it is for the people He created to create, own and possess financial wealth, to have the power which He is ever willing to give to every man who shall make choice to be rich that he might be able to create financial wealth and live in possession of riches.

"For the poor will never cease from the land..." (Deut.15v11). God certainly knew that many of the poor will ever be living among the rich in every land. Why? Because God knows the end from the beginning; He knew that those

people who shall allow themselves to remain in bondage to Satan's lies and deception will certainly be poor in life. So, God is right for saying that these set of people who shall by their choice remain poor will never cease in the land. Not that God had created certain set of people to be poor. But if you make a choice to be poor He would respect your choice.

"I returned and saw under the sun that – Nor riches to men of understanding ... But time and chance happen to them all" *(Ecc.9v10)*. It took the uncommon wisdom of God for King Solomon to understand the truth that no man is created to be poor. According to him there are no set of people with any special advantage of understanding whom God had created to be rich. To every man He has created, God has given the same and equal playing ground of 'Time and Chance' to create financial wealth in life. A time (moment) and a chance (opportunity) to be rich in life would always come to everyone created by God.

That's to say, that there is a moment of opportunity that God offers or brings to everyone to be rich. But once you have made your choice to be poor in life, you will definitely not be rich even when you have a time and a chance to be rich. People who allow this rare moment of opportunity to slip off their hands are those who have made a choice to be poor. There is no poor man today who have not once had a time and a chance (a moment of opportunity) in his life to be rich. But such a man who is poor today has decided not to utilize his moment of opportunity to be rich because he had yesterday already made a choice to be poor in life.

Man has continued to be helpless in his choice to be poor, and desperately needed God's help. At the appointed time, Christ came in God's fullness of GRACE to offer grace – God's help to enable man become rich once again. Christ being the second Adam, made a choice on behalf of the entire human race to become poor that every man might through His poverty once again become rich.

"For you know the grace of our Lord Jesus Christ, that though He was rich, yet for your sake He became poor, that you through His poverty you might become rich" (2Cor.8v9). Christ wasn't in any way under any duress or compulsion to become poor. According to divine purpose, Christ's choice to become poor was totally a deliberate one supposedly to affirm the fact that to be poor is a choice. Though Christ having taken the human form did make a choice to become poor on earth, yet He is greatly rich as the Son of God whose everlasting great riches of financial wealth are immeasurably endless. This is why we who now believed in Him as God's only begotten Son could through His poverty become rich only by God's power and by your choice.

Satan has today craftily and cunningly diversified his lies and deceptions in a man's mind. These diversified lies and deceptions of Satan are better called 'the lies and deceptions of the mind'. By man's great fall from glory through sin, man has opened up his mind to become Satan's workshop where he now manufactures and stocks up his lies and deceptions by which he has continued to influence many to make a choice to be poor in life. With these diversified lies and deceptions of the mind, many people including most Christians are today living with a negative mindset or shift of position in mind. All those people living with this negative mindset are obviously poor because they have allowed the lies and deceptions stocked in their mind to affect their choice-making decision to create financial wealth and walk away from poverty in life.

By definition, mindset is the position of a man's mind over a period of time that determines his attitude, thinking pattern, idea, belief and actions which is often difficult to change. Your mindset can either be positive or negative depending on what you allow to position your mind. Once you allow the lies and deceptions of the mind to make a negative position or setting of your mind, then you will be influenced by them to make a choice to be poor in life. In this case, the lies and deceptions of the mind which is of Satan will control you to believe that you can't be rich in life; as well as not to take necessary actions to create financial wealth. As soon as you accept the idea of believing that you can't be rich, you will equally decide not to take any action to be rich. And eventually you may never be, once you have obviously been influenced to make a choice to be poor.

You have got to believe that you can create financial wealth for yourself to get out of poverty to live a rich life. Because you are after all destined for it. Never should you have a negative mindset that you can't create financial wealth. If you think so, that's your choice. But remember that as a man thinks in his heart so he is *(Prvb.23v7)*.

Long term success of creating financial wealth isn't accomplished by a man with a negative mindset about becoming rich. Even God will not change people's condition until they change their old-thinking and old-mind value system. You may never become rich in life not until you change your negative mindset and positively get your mind re-set and repositioned. There are many millionaires and billionaires today who were born into poverty and struggled through it, but they ended up adjusting their negative mindset and eventually turned their lives around. Today they had become an inspiration to anyone who is dreaming of becoming successful in one's professional career as a means of livelihood for creating financial wealth. Celine Dion was born to a French-Canadian family of 14 children. Her parents struggled to provide for her and her siblings when they were growing up. But Celine Dion's choice not to be poor in life was what made the big difference for her.

"When you have money, your friends know who you are. When you have no money, you know who your friends are" – *Cam Mi Pham, Vietnam born personal development blogger.* You don't have to choose to be poor to know who your friends are. You better make a choice to be rich, so that people who shall know the worth of your financial wealth would become your friends.

Lies and Deceptions that can influence your choice to be poor?

Below are the eleven lies and deceptions of the mind which are from Satan that can influence you to make a choice to be poor in life.

Superstitious ancestral belief: Certain people believe that poverty runs in their ancestry. Such people do believe that they can't be rich in life too because their parents, grand and great grandparents were all poor during their life time. This is one of the greatest lies and deceptions of the mind by which Satan has continued to enslave a lot of people to remain in poverty. So long as you are holding onto this superstitious ancestral belief which is a mere lie and deception of the mind, you may never become rich in life. Superstitious ancestral belief about poverty is a shackle you must break off your life. Until you lose yourself free from the shackle of this lie and deception of the mind you may never be free from living in poverty.

Death of a bread winner: Your chance of becoming rich in life is not in the hands of your bread winner. Neither can the death of your bread winner stop you in life from becoming rich. Rather it is your choice to make, either to become rich or poor. Listen, the death of your bread winner can't be enough reason that would make you not to become rich except if you choose to. Your bread winner could either be your parent, uncle, wife, husband, son or daughter, brother or sister, priest or pastor, or a Good Samaritan. Whoever he may be, it is a lie and deception of the mind for you to believe that you can't make it to be rich in life because you lost your bread winner to death. If you believe that the death of your bread winner could mark the end of your prospect to become rich in life, then you have just believed but a lie and deception of the mind.

Not being educated: To become rich in life is never in any way reserved only for the educated. It is a complete lie and deception should you believe that you can't make it to become rich in life simply because you are not educated. Among the world's most men of riches today, there are many who were never educated. At least *Jerry John Rawlings* who once was president of Ghana never had a graduate degree, yet he is today one of the riches people in his native country. *Bill Gates* of America was a dropout from school yet he refused to believe this lie and deception of the mind that he won't be rich in life. Today as one of the world's richest men, he has proved that not being educated shouldn't be a reason for anyone's choice to be poor in life. The uneducated can be rich just as the educated can. It's all about your choice to make.

One African among others proved it all that not being educated is not a reason to be poor in life. Innocent Chukwuma Ifediaso, is a multi-million dollar Nigerian entrepreneur. He unfortunately could not acquire a university degree but ended up with high school education only. But today, he is the owner and CEO of Innoson Motors and Group of Companies. His company is hosting the biggest vehicle assembling plant owned by any single individual in the whole of African continent with the brand name (IVM) Innoson Vehicle Manufacturing. Besides assembling different model of buses, Hilux van, trucks and other vehicles, Innoson Motors and Group of Companies is also manufacturing and exporting motorcycles, tricycles, spare parts, tyres, and all manner of designed plastic utensils and containers that worth millions of dollars.

Inferiority complex: Certain other persons on earth do wrongly believe that they are inferior species of human beings who ultimately are not created to be rich in life.

They are more comfortable and contented with being poor than becoming rich. They prefer poverty to riches. Give these people the options of being rich and poor. They will still make the choice to be poor. Why? Because they believe in this lie and deception of the mind which makes them to see themselves as being so inferior compared with those that are rich. These set of people see poverty as being more suitable for them than riches would be for them. For them they conclude they are already unlucky that they can't be rich anymore. Because to them God created some people to be rich and some others to be poor. Therefore, they believe they are among those created to be poor of which they do accept to be their lot. But is God a partial God? No!

Ignorance of human potentials: Nothing else except a lie and deception of the mind could make you believe that you don't have the potentials to become rich in life. God doesn't create any human who is empty of the potentials to be rich. Right within inside of you, you are equipped with customized potentials to become rich. But you may never become rich in life not until you discover your innate potentials. Of course you should fully take advantage of your endowed potentials as much as you discover them. Yours could be your passion or interest, gift or talent, inspiring ideas, creative thinking or ability, acquired knowledge or experience, etc. Truly you have the required human potentials that you could harness to become rich. Your potentials are the first great resources that you actually need to put into use if you really want to become rich. The rich you know don't have two human heads but one just as you. The rich simply do believed that they have the potentials to be rich. And they made the right moves to hit it big. So, for you to believe that you don't have what it takes to become rich is completely a lie and deception of the mind.

Religious belief: Also, people do make their choice to be poor in life because of their religious belief. There are some religious movements whose belief advocates for poverty than for riches. Note that no foundation of any religion or its doctrinal origination and practice is higher than God Himself nor can change God's will for man to be rich. God at creation revealed this awesome will for man when He put and positioned Adam to live continually inside of the Eden Garden full of God's immeasurable glorious riches including financial wealth. Obviously it could only have been God who alone is an embodiment of everlasting immeasurable abundant financial wealth, whose will it is for man to be rich, to have made a Garden that was a true replica of His embodied riches in financial wealth inside of which He personally put and positioned Man (Adam) to continually live, possess and control them.

If your religious belief holds that man is not created to be rich, then does it mean that God as the creator of man is poor too? If your religious belief holds that riches is evil, then does it mean that God who is an embodiment of great riches in financial wealth is evil too? If you conclude that your religious belief is right in its position that men or some men are not created to be rich, then may be God was wrong to put Adam in the Garden of Eden. And maybe it was a coincident that the patriarchs of faith – Abraham, Isaac, Jacob, David who worked with God were all rich men, having created financial wealth. It was after the fall of Adam when men began to believe the lie and deception of Satan instead of God's truth and knowledge that the poor among men began to emerge. The choice is still yours to make!

Government's breach of expectations: Government can't make choice for you to become rich in life. But government can only provide you with an enabling environment or platform that could help you to become rich. There is no other better enabling environment than what could be called the electorate or public expectations from the government. These may include: provision of employment, steady power supply, good roads, affordable and quality education, entrepreneurial skill acquisition institutions or centres, soft credit facilities, pro-economic growth and development policies and programs, stability and social security, democratization and justice value system, etc.

Often than not, government do breach these expectations because of their inability to provide them perhaps for any reason beyond their control or for reason of corruption.

Your chances to become rich with 100% dependency on government to meet your expectation is extremely less. It is a great lie and deception of the mind to think that you can't be rich because government has failed to meet with your expectations. Government's breach of expectation shouldn't influence you to make a choice to be poor. Even when government falls short of your expectations, you can still become rich in life. But that's if you choose to. Listen, even in the least less developing countries where governments had woefully failed to meet with these public expectations, yet there are great number of millionaire and billionaire rich men who out of nothing are still creating, owning and possessing financial wealth. Just because they made their choice not to be poor.

Being a victim of life tragedy: Being a victim of any of the life tragedies isn't enough to influence you to make a choice to be poor in life. In life anyone can accidentally become a victim of any life tragedies such as fire outbreak, flood incident, robbery attack, fraud or scam, sickness or disease, fatal accident, war and violent crisis, etc. Truly either of these tragedies of life can result to loss of your business, investment, money, time, property, resources, health, etc. Yet you can still become rich in life even though you may have lost your business, investment, money or property to any of these tragedies of life. To believe that you can't become rich in life because you are facing or had faced any of these tragedies of life is a pure lie and deception of the mind. And once you believe this lie and deception of the mind then it would influence you to make a choice to be poor in life instead of becoming rich. Many people across the globe were once victims of these life tragedies. A great number of them virtually lost everything they had during the tragedy but today they are people of great financial wealth.

The runners up by name Kechi, in the 2017 American Got Talent Show, was a victim of a tragic plane crash that claimed the lives of the passengers on board except her and one other. Despite severe burnt all over her body, delay in her academic studies and psychological trauma experience, she was not deterred and refused to allow her life tragedy to influence her to make a choice to be poor in life. Rather, she has since put it behind her, pursued her university studies, and at the talent show she had proved to the world that she could usefully engage her discovered talent to create financial wealth than to choose to be poor in life.

Being physically challenged: To be physically challenged is not a chance to change your choice to become poor in life. Don't ever allow this lie and deception of the mind to make you believe that you can't become rich in life simply because you are physically challenged. I am sure that those who are rich are never rich because they are not physically challenged. They are rich because they had a positive mindset about becoming rich and made their choice to become one. Therefore, it is never your physically challenged status that would make you become poor in life. Rather, it is your negative mindset about your status of being physically challenged that can make you become poor. Once you allow this lie and deception of the mind to give you a negative mindset, then it would influence you to make a choice to be poor in life. All because you have allowed this lie and deception of the mind to make you think that a physically challenged person can't be able any longer to become rich. But I do know and have come across certain wealthy and rich physically challenged people among whom is even a state law maker, a business executive, a high ranking public worker, a senior lecturer, etc.

Experience of failure: You shouldn't make your experience of failure in life to become a lie and deception in your mind. If you do, it could influence you to make a choice to be poor in life. That you have failed many a times in life is not a reason for you to believe that you can't anymore become rich. Don't be deterred by your failure experiences in life. Failure doesn't signify poverty. Nor can failure make you become a poor man. But you can allow failure to influence you to choose to be poor. Many who are rich today had failed several times in life before they eventually became rich. Where you had failed you will eventually succeed only if you maintain a positive mindset that you can. Failure is not a license to become poor in life but a lesson to position yourself better to successfully become rich. So, don't allow your profile of failure experiences to influence you to make the wrong choice to be poor in life.

Laziness and Idleness: It won't be long if you are lazy that you would decide to be idle. Poverty is a close associate of laziness and idleness. Even God condemns laziness and idleness. *"A little sleep, a little slumber, a little folding of the hands to sleep – so shall your poverty come on you like a prowler… He who has a slack hand becomes poor, but the hand of the diligent makes rich" (Prvb.6v10, 10v4)*. It is a negative mindset shaped with a great lie and deception to think that you can be lazy and idle, and still become rich in life. Not at all. It could only be a day dream in mirage. No lazy and idle man has ever become rich in life not even by lottery. In fact, you really need to reset and reposition your mind from the lie and deception that you can be lazy and idle in life, and still hope to be rich. This negative mindset can only get you frustrated in life and eventually influence you to hopelessly surrender to making a choice to be poor.

Extravagant habit and lifestyle: Your consistent thoughts would always give birth to your consistent confession. What you confess all the time soon becomes your action. Your actions over a period of time becomes your habit. And your habit develops to become your character. The character you live with over a period of time eventually becomes your lifestyle. Both habit and lifestyle are two extremes of character that are always too strong to change. To think you can be rich in life with an extravagant habit and lifestyle is a serious negative mindset. It has never worked out for anyone who has lived that way because it is great lie and deception of the mind.

Spending every of your penny or income wastefully or extravagantly on frivolous things and unneedful luxuries is an express route to bankruptcy and invitation of poverty. Such frivolous things could include grooving and partying, hosting societal burial, wedding and other social ceremonies, hard drug consumption, etc. Also such unneedful luxuries may include display of latest model of posh cars, rental of first class apartment, purchase of most expensive designer's wears and shoes and jewelries, especially when they are unmatchable with your current income. Indulging in this extravagant habit and lifestyle most a times is only for the mere sake of gaining social attraction and popularity.

Unfortunately, many who once were million dollar rich

men that gave themselves to extravagant habit and lifestyle later became either bankrupt or pitiably poor in life. For instance, some notable American music rappers who once were millionaires were later in life declared bankrupt, while others are now living a lowly poor life. Also, the Brazilian football legend, Adriano who once was a rich millionaire later became a poor drug addict living in a suburb ghetto near the city of Rio de Janeiro in Brazil, obviously because of his extravagant habit and lifestyle. You would obviously be disappointed and frustrated if you think you can hold on to your extravagant habit and lifestyle, and still become rich in life. And once you allow this mindset to control you, you may be frustrated and consequently be influenced to choose to be poor in life.

Consequences of Poverty

Dishonor and neglect: Poverty no doubt brings dishonor and neglect. A poor man is accommodated and welcomed but may not be honored. A poor man is normally neglected even when he has great ideas to offer or useful contributions to make. People never considers the poor to be relevant. The poor is often seen as not only being less privileged but also as second class citizens. The poor are usually relegated to the background in the society especially when it comes to the state affairs and scheme of things. The poor are never allowed to occupy positions of honor in the society.

Inability to afford basic needs: The greatest of all the consequences of poverty is the inability to afford the basic needs of life which include: food, clothing, shelter and comfort facilities. Poverty exposes you to hunger, famine, and malnutrition which eventually may lead to death. The poor struggles to put food on his table. Even when the poor can, it would be junks which may not even make up to three square meals per day. The word dietary becomes a deliberate omission in their feeding dictionary. Their clothing are full of stocks of inferior clothes that could better be used as rags. The poor are the legitimate residents of ghettos, suburbs or thatched apartments within the cities. The poor lacks the taste of living in comfort. Imagine a family of seven living just in one room apartment; never had opportunity to lay their bodies on good matrass but on mat; never had the opportunity to put on fan no matter the heat; never had opportunity to drink chilled water no matter the hot weather; never had opportunity to cook food with stove or gas but with firewood no matter how tired they may be; etc. This condition of life described an absence of comfort facilities. These are what the poor suffers.

Psychological torture: Poverty is associated with psychological torture. The poor is always psychologically tortured with pain and agony in the heart. Sometimes poverty can limit happiness and leaves the mind traumatized with the feeling of being poor. Poverty afflicts the heart with a feeling of un-fulfilment in life. This psychological torture caused by poverty can affect the health of the poor. Poverty adds more pressure on the poor for survival which could weary the mind and cause a total body breakdown.

Cycling of generational poverty: To be poor in life is not a sin if that's your choice; but to transfer poverty to your children and their future generations is a curse. And this is one of the great consequences of poverty. If you choose to be poor in life, be mindful that your poverty can cycle down to your next generations. If you don't make a choice today to be rich so as to end poverty in your life; then how sure are you that your children would be rich? The probability is that if you end up being poor in life; your children after you may equally be poor in life too. Except if your children or one of them eventually breaks the jinx of the poverty by making a choice to create financial wealth to become rich. The fact is that poverty begets poverty and riches begets riches. You have the right to make a choice either to lay a cycling foundation of generational poverty or riches. Should you choose to be poor in life, you may face the consequence of leaving behind a cycling of generational poverty.

Envy and jealousy: Poverty breeds envy and jealousy in the heart of the poor. The poor because of his poverty becomes envious and jealous of the rich. With a poverty-caused envy and jealousy, the heart of the poor could be flooded with evil thoughts usually aimed to take undue advantage either to bring down the rich or dispossess the rich of his riches in order to have a glimpse taste of it. Such evil thoughts may include to go and rob, kidnap, defraud, and sometimes to kill the rich, just to get their money to become rich. You can't afford to be poor in life to live with envy and jealousy. Because envy signifies regret while jealousy signifies defeat. If you make a choice to be poor in life; when you see or meet with the rich you immediately become regretful of being poor. Also, you feel defeated for not being rich. You better choose not to be poor so that you don't live with lifelong feeling of regret and defeat that comes with poverty.

Slave to the rich: Poverty is the only credential that automatically qualifies the poor to become a life time slave to the rich. Poverty is greatest backbone of slavery. While the rich is the master, the poor is the slave-servant. The poor is generally at the service of the rich. The greater part of the work or job that the poor does for survival is provided by the rich. That's to say, the rich determines the income of the poor. Of course, you know the rich would never pay the poor a sustainable income. They work and labor much for the rich but receive less from them. The great potentials, ideas, strength and energy of the poor are enslaved and completely tapped by the rich to continually build their empire of financial wealth. You must ask yourself, is this what I really want for myself? If your answer is no, then you should equally say no to poverty. Make your choice today to be rich in life, and not to be poor so that you won't live to be a slave to the rich.

Oppression and intimidation: Poverty is a ticket that can allow the poor to suffer oppression and intimidation in the hands of the rich. The rich among themselves can only battle or rock horn with one another but not necessarily to oppress or intimidate one another. Because each of the rich has a level of financial ability to defend himself against the other, unlike the poor who has not. Poverty can make the poor to live in the shadow of fear of the rich. The financial wealth of the riches creates space for them to exercise dominion. Of course, the only territory that the rich can dominate is the territory of the poor. In the territory of the poor, the rich do find enough space to oppress and intimidate the poor with little or no resistance. The poor is never in opposition to the rich but is oppressed by the rich. Nor is the rich interrogated by the poor rather the poor is intimidated by the rich. It is left for you to decide on which choice to make, whether to be poor or rich in life. Don't forget, the choice you make is what will determine your financial ability.

CHAPTER EIGHT

WHY YOU NEED TO CREATE FINANCIAL WEALTH

You are an art-craft-creator

Truly, you are an art-craft-creator delegated by God to create financial wealth for your daily survival, sustenance of life and security against poverty. As an art-craft-creator whom God has made, He made available to you 'the will power'; 'the capital resources' – brain, talent and time enveloped with opportunities; as well as 'revelation and wisdom for knowledge'. These are all that you need as a creator to effectively and successfully create financial wealth to live a rich life. But if you fail to create financial wealth, you may never live in riches.

Of course, creating financial wealth requires hard-work. Financial wealth is the end resource that becomes a means for you to become a man of riches. As a child of God, you are created not to be poor. Because for your sake, Christ had become poor that you may be rich. God is the ultimate creator who in the nature of His same image after His likeness has created you too to be an art-craft creator of all good things that life requires among which is financial wealth.

Who is a rich-wealthy person?

You are a rich-wealthy person only if you are currently in the art-craft process of creating financial wealth , either by being actively engaged in a career job, operating a self-owned business, possessing acquired material and financial assets or property, and or owning an established business investments from which you earn periodic monetary income or returns to be financially independent, abundant and able to afford the basic needs or necessities of life; to offer yourself the needed comfort in life; to provide impactful need-based help and assistance to improve the welfare and wellbeing of the poor and needy; to support God's kingdom work; to support community development projects; and to continually take advantage of newly emerging business and investment opportunities for more job creations not only to hire the unemployed labour force in the society to work for you in order for them to be earning a steady periodic income pay for their own financial survival and livelihood; but also to further diversify and expand your income earnings or returns for a continuous financial wealth creation and sustenance.

As a dimension of prosperity, until you begin to create financial wealth, you are never rich. And unless you become financially independent, abundant and able, you may not afford to provide yourself with the basic needs or necessities of life, to offer yourself the needed comfort in life not necessarily the luxuries and affluence of living; to provide impactful support to God's kingdom work; to offer a need-based social welfare assistance and help to others; to support strategic community development projects; to acquire valuable material and financial assets; to establish or own businesses and investments; and to hire or employ other people in the society.

In a nutshell I have provided you with a clear picture of what it all means for it to be said that one is a rich-wealthy person. Have you attained to this height in life, if yes, it then means you have actually become financially independent, abundant and able. But if no, then it means you have not actually created enough financial wealth for yourself.

The rich-wealthy people are those with greater financial ability. You can't own and possess financial wealth without riches at your disposal. And a man of great financial wealth lives to enjoy riches. No one creates financial wealth only by dreaming for it. You create financial wealth that you desire to own and possess in order to be rich enough to raise your financial ability to a higher level.

And without being rich you won't have the financial ability to afford for yourself the basic needs of life required to take good care of your body; to live a quality, comfortable, and impactful life while on earth. Remember, financial wealth with all that it encompasses is not alone prosperity but is only a dimension of it.

The benefits of owning and possessing financial wealth

Now that you have known what it takes to say that a person is rich in financial wealth, it is also imperative that you understand the benefits of financial wealth ownership and possession.

Financial ability to do the needful purpose:

To have financial ability to do the needful purpose is one of the benefits of owning and possessing financial wealth. Unfortunately there has been a wrongly misconception today among the people of great financial wealth about why they are owning and possessing it in life. *"Not that we are sufficient of ourselves to think of anything as being from ourselves, but our sufficiency is from God" (2Cor.3v5).* If your financial sufficiency is truly from God who alone made it possible, certainly it is for a needful purpose. Of course, God does not want you to create, own and possesses financial wealth only for a self-centered purpose. No! Therefore, the needful purpose which is the main benefit of creating, owning and possessing financial wealth is to have the financial ability:

    a.   To provide the basic daily and immediate future needs or necessities of life for yourself, your home, your family, and or for others *(Math.6v25-32, Ph.4v19).* Creating, owning and possessing financial wealth offers you the financial ability to afford quality food; and to afford standard shelter to live in; to afford quality clothes for your clothing.

b. To provide yourself with needful comfort facilities *(Ph.4v19)* and not for luxuries in life. Creating, owning and possessing financial wealth offers you the financial ability to afford the basic needful comfort facilities that life requires for convenience and easy-made living.

c. To acquire valuable assets or property, and make viable and profitable business investments *(2Chr.17v13)*. Creating, owning and possessing financial wealth affords you the financial ability to acquire income-yielding material and financial assets or property, and establish profitable business investments to expand and diversify income earnings or returns for continuous financial wealth creation and sustenance of riches

d. To finance and support humanitarian cause and social work services *(Deut.15v11, Math.25v31-46)*. Creating, owning and possessing financial wealth gives you the financial ability to finance and support life-changing humanitarian cause and people-oriented social work services aimed at improving on the welfare and bettering the lives of others especially the poor and needy as a way of demonstrating God's love.

e. To finance and support God's kingdom work *(Luk.8v1-3)*. Creating, owning and possessing financial wealth offers you the financial ability to finance and support God's kingdom work and project so as to help get His will done on earth as it is done in heaven to the glory of God's name.

f. To finance and support community development projects *(Chr.17v12)*. Creating, owning and possessing financial wealth also offers you the financial ability to finance and support strategic community development projects aimed at bringing positive economic impact and growth capable of enhancing societal development for the progress of all. To support this fact, someone says, *"The truly rich people think about serving others and giving back to the community. The currency of real networking is not greed but generosity"*.

The utmost benefit of creating, owning and possessing financial wealth is to have the financial ability to bring hope, help, happiness and motivation not just to yourself but also to others around you especially those whom you are more privileged than. To own and possess financial wealth is not to lavish your riches and the monetary proceeds from your wealth creation only for your own selfish satisfaction and luxury living just for a show of pride and extravagance. Remember, *"Whatever we do for ourselves die with us but what we do for others and the world remains, and is immortal"* – Albert Pine.

Control of power: Another great benefit of creating, owning and possessing financial wealth is that it gives you access to command both the politicking-economic and financial power. Financial wealth ownership and possession do wields you the politicking-economic and financial power: To rule over poverty and escape its attendant consequences of being dishonored and neglected, of the inability to do the needful purpose, of undergoing psychological torture, of cycling generational poverty, of unnecessarily becoming jealous and envy of the rich, of being a slave to the rich, of being oppressed and intimidated by the rich; To take advantage of emerging business and investment opportunities to create more financial wealth and become wealthier, to survive inflation and recession tough times without being a hard-hit victim, to comfortably take care of unforeseen and precautionary emergencies that may occur or arise, and to maintain continually the choice of a living standard that best suits your self-ego or personality profile; To gain social recognition, to command influence and to earn followership from the public. In fact, great financial wealth ownership and possession is the only non-people electorate that gives you the politicking ability to gain social relevance, to command influence and to earn followership to your own benefit. In favor of the fact that money answers all things, a poor man is to a large extent often considered to be socially irrelevant. Besides a man's profile of good name and his positive societal impact, financial wealth ownership and possession is another sure way of gaining social relevance. When you have the economic and financial power that financial wealth ownership and possession accords, you also have the politicking ability to command influence over people to your own advantage and to earn their followership to your own benefit.

Earning of honor and respect: When you own and possess financial wealth, people around you honor and respect you. Within the societal structure, the rich are never bound to force but to earn honor or respect from the poor. The poor are never financially indebted to the rich yet they are in debt of honor and respect to them simply because the rich are owners of financial wealth. As a mark of honor and respect, the poor are ever willing to serve the rich even in their inconvenience, to spend their time free of charge for the rich just to please them, offer their seats to the rich in official gatherings, and to offer themselves to work tirelessly for the rich in anticipation of a reward in return. Once you own and possess financial wealth; when you step out in any gathering and make a speech before men, men would applaud with a standing ovation, all as a mark of honor and respect.

Gaining of fame: Automatically, owning and possessing great financial wealth gains you fame but most especially if you are actively involved in making positive impact on the lives of people around you or advancing any life-impacting cause for the progress of humanity. Financial wealth ownership and possession gains you fame beyond your territorial resident. People everywhere farther than your current place of dwelling get to know you sometimes without even having to meet you. The more your financial wealth gains you fame, the more you get more fans whom you may unknowingly be inspiring to become rich to get out of poverty.

Acquisition of connections and contacts: Financial wealth ownership and possession enables you to make and establish relevant connections and contacts in the society. There are certain connections and contacts that you may never build or establish as a poor person except if you are rich in life. Highly worth personal connections and social contacts are necessary that you should have them, even though God sometimes do reveal Himself higher to relegate them to nothing. Acquiring connections and contacts via financial wealth ownership and possession is imperative because through them you can get what you want, get help for yourself or for someone else of your choice, get things done faster without much protocol, get decisions influenced to your favor, and get the direction or flow of things changed to suit you best. Once you have become wealthy and rich in life, you become connected with the highly placed men and women in the society; the Who is who, the bourgeois, influential juggernauts, distinguished career professionals, political and economic rulers whose contacts with you become useful asset to you.

Preferential rights with personal privileges: Financial wealth ownership and possession would automatically make you legitimate to enjoy certain preferential rights and privileges. These preferential rights and privileges, the poor may never enjoy them. Financial wealth ownership and possession would always place you in a lifted position where political office holders, financial institutions wherein you do business, some educational institutions, churches or religious bodies, your host community, and including the poor too will be out rightly willing without negotiation to offer you certain preferential rights with personal privileges as way to celebrate you for your financial wealth.

Feeling of self-fulfillment: Yes, as a Christian, it is a fact that neither being poor nor rich would determine your eternal heavenly destination hereafter. Yet, no matter how hopeful or certain you are, to make heaven where none shall anymore be poor or live in poverty; still no such hope or certainty as long as you are poor or living in poverty while here on earth will be enough to give you complete feeling of self-fulfillment. When you personally create, own and possess financial wealth, it gives you feeling of self-fulfillment. In this case, you obviously live with a bit sense of self-actualization and personal satisfaction in life. Nothing else can give you feeling of self-fulfillment and self-arrival in life, than financial wealth especially if complimented with an assurance of eternal hope of glory in heaven hereafter.

CHAPTER NINE

FINANCIAL WEALTH DEFINES FINANCIAL ABILITIES

Categories of financial ability

As a core benefit, the greatest financial parameter to measure financial wealth is the financial ability or inability of a man to afford the basic needs or necessities of life – (food, shelter, clothing); to offer yourself needful comfort facilities in life not necessarily the luxury facilities for affluent living; to provide impactful support to God's kingdom work; to offer a need-based social welfare assistance and help to others; to support strategic community development projects; to acquire valuable material and financial assets; to establish or own businesses and investments; and to hire or employ other people in the society in order for them to have a means of livelihood.

However, there are four basic categories to measure the financial ability of people living on earth. No one is living on earth that does not belong to either of these categories. Neither has anyone ever lived in the duality of these categories at the same time. Capacity determines ability. Your financial wealth gives you financial capacity. And your financial capacity determines your financial ability. Your financial ability determines what you can provide; the level of impact you can make; what you can acquire or own; and the extent you can hire others to work for you to earn a living. These categories of financial ability of people include:

Financial ability of the paupers

Whenever you are not able to provide for yourself the following basic needs of life which include: food, clothing, and shelter. By this reality you are therefore categorized as a member of **the paupers** whose financial ability is at the **zero point** cadre.

Unfortunately, these categories of people whose financial ability is at zero point do live as beggars. They are always found in every part of the continents of the world. Irrespective of the parts of the continent of the world where they may be found, they are not always completely different from one another. Whether these people are in the south or west and north or east continents of the world, the paupers do have in common the same financial ability. The most common among this category is that by their level of financial ability they cannot afford or provide themselves with the basic necessities or needs of life – food, clothing and shelter. With their level of financial ability they can't afford three square meals a day; they don't have enough clothes not even fairly used ones to clothe their nakedness; they live in rickety or thatched houses often located in the most poverty stricken rural communities; they completely lack comfort facilities in life. Most a times they have no job whether paid or self-employed or anything else that they do as a source of income.

Any day you find yourself not being able any longer to afford these basic needs of life will mark the day that your poverty as a pauper will begin. And it won't be long that you may soon even turn out to become a beggar. Unfortunately, if you ever become a beggar you will eventually begin to live a beggarly life. Hence you will join the global league of those who have no financial ability at all to live and survive. Then others may begin to address you as a helpless and hopeless financial dependent. Unfortunately, most of their children either do not always go to school, do end up as school drop-outs or do end up as working servants in the house of the rich.

They are financially dependent mostly on others such as their parents, relatives, friends and sometimes good spirited-individuals for their continued survival. The financial inability of these paupers do leave them with no option than to either depend on others or struggle in suffering to feed, clothe and shelter themselves. Of course these paupers category of people are not really the beggars and lunatics or mad people who could be found in the streets or corners of most cities and towns. Rather they are those who unfortunately have been influence by either of the lies and deceptions of the mind not to create financial wealth to become rich but remain poor.

Also, they are those who have failed to discover or learn the strategies and principles of financial wealth creation that they needed to apply to become rich. By implication of the above failure they eventually have made themselves brothers and associates of the streets' lunatics and beggars. The obvious difference between these two is that while the paupers do have tattered or indecent home (a place of shelter) the beggars and lunatics or mad people may not but loiter and live on the streets. Make sure you don't belong to these paupers category of people whose financial ability is the least. You don't deserve to be one of them.

The Poor

The poor are the category of people whose financial ability is at the **lowest point**. The financial ability of the poor can only enable them to afford the basic needs of life, but such that are of low in quality and of sub-standard, with a great struggle to afford the basic comfort facilities that they may need in life such as modern good looking apartment, mobility of any kind, electronics and home appliances, etc. These categories of people who are poor are almost living in every part of the world.

The poor people do lack the financial ability to live a

quality, better and enhanced life. They struggle to make savings out of their poor income. Mostly they do borrow and often live in debt which they struggle to offset. They lack the financial ability to make any commendable financial impact on others around them or in their society. Mostly the poor do engage themselves either in menial self-provided or paid jobs. Sometimes the jobs they do are often not steady, and such does not guarantee even a steady minimal income in some cases. These poor categories of people do send their children to the lowest affordable schools around.

Both the paupers and the poor together are the nobodies in the society. No one cares to take notice of them let alone respecting them. The paupers and the poor are the categories of the people in the society whom the rich and men of riches do refer as the less privileged. Most a times they are the victims of oppression by the ungodly rich and men of riches. You can really get yourself out of these zero and lower point of financial ability in life.

The Rich-Poor

These are the category of people whose financial ability is at the **average point**. Just like the paupers and the poor, the rich-poor are also everywhere in every part of the world. These category of people are neither poor nor rich. The rich-poor do have the financial ability to afford the basic needs or necessities of life but also still struggle to afford most of the basic comfort facilities they needed in life. At ease they can actually afford to feed on average quality food at least for three times a day; afford to live in a modern good-looking place of shelter; afford an average quality clothing to clothe themselves; and afford to moderately provide themselves with some of the basic comfort facilities they mostly needed in life as mentioned earlier above.

Equally the poor-rich in most cases do have reserves of little savings from which they can take care of precautionary emergencies. At such unexpected emergency cases, their reserves of savings sometimes are not always enough for them, hence they do turn out to borrowing and sometimes live in debt. The poor-rich category of people do engage themselves either in an average income yielding self-employment or in an average paid job. They can only boost of having the financial ability to live a bettered average and enhanced life. They can make only a little commendable financial impact in the lives of others around them. Yet the poor-rich still lack the financial ability to acquire to their possession high valuable financial and material assets and or investment. Considering their financial ability, these rich-poor category of people can afford to send their children either to below average or averagely affordable schools around.

The Rich

These are the category of people whose financial ability is at **high point**. The rich are obviously everywhere in every city, region, nation and continent of the world. The rich are mostly the people occupying high income paying political offices, employees of high income paying jobs, owners of high income yielding business investments or financial assets and other high income earning professionals. As a matter of fact the rich do have the financial ability to afford at ease the best of all the basic necessities of life with access to adequate comfort facilities in life: they can conveniently afford as many quality square meals or delicacies as possible for them and their entire family; they can afford the best of designers' clothes at the market.

The rich too have the financial ability to acquire, possess and control at least certain valuable financial and material assets and or business investment which places them in position as employers of labor up to a minimum of 50 but less than 500 people in their payroll who work for them to earn a living; to offer commendable financial help and support to others around and to the society as much as they can and wish to offer.

Such valuable financial and material assets and business investments they do acquire, possess and control may include: financial assets such as stocks, bonds, debentures, treasury bills; material assets such as real estate and landed property; and investment assets such as business establishment, company, etc. To these category of people their main focus in life is no longer on how to afford the basic needs and comfort facilities in life but on how to acquire to their ownership, possession and control of more financial assets, material assets and investment assets. The rich's financial ability enable them have reasonable or huge reserve of savings from which they can without any worry take care of any arising accidental expenses and or precautionary emergencies. They are entitle to a large sum of returnable income flow from their assets and investments, either on daily, weekly, monthly or yearly basis. These assets and investment are usually scattered within the rich's country of residence but sometimes in abroad too.

The rich are the big time customers of the banks to whom the banks do offer preferential treatment. For investment purposes, they transact a lot with the banks and sometimes do actually borrow huge money from them either to take advantage of an available new investment opportunity or to finance their already existing business investment. This they do mostly through bank loans and overdrafts facilities. In other words, it is often on this ground only that the rich can either incur or live in debt but never because of any personal expenses. The rich do have access to a higher than average income flow usually from more than one source. They can boost of having the financial ability to live a comfortable and enhanced quality life.

The rich are the categories of people that have the financial ability to get richer in the society more than a good number of others. Because considering their financial ability they are better positioned everyday than the paupers, the poor and the rich-poor to always take advantage of any available investment opportunities. These rich category of people do have the financial ability to send their children to high cost or expensive schools where they can acquire high quality education. The rich do own the best of cars. Most of their trips are by air route with the best airlines as first class passengers. But less often than not they do board flight as economy class passengers for those of them that are quite humble.

The rich do have their own private experts virtually in every profession such as doctor, lawyer, accountant etc. who renders professional service to them and their family. Also, they do have maid servants and other auxiliary house workers who render services to them such as drivers, cooks, gardeners, security men, cleaners, etc. The rich do wield and command power and influence especially in their resident state, province or region of a country and most a times across the state, province, or region but within their country. They live in their own millions' worth mansion mostly situated in the choicest areas of any city where they are residing. Most of these rich people are directly or indirectly into state politics. They do have a good number of political friends and loyalists, sometimes political candidates whom they sponsor for various political offices.

The Men of riches

These are the category of people whose financial ability is at the **extreme or excessive point**. Within the circumference of financial wealth, men of riches are the billionaires. The men of riches are the categories of people on earth whose financial ability is at the excessive point when compared with the rich, the rich-poor, the poor, and the paupers. These men of riches are not too many but few in every nation of the world. In common the men of riches do have the financial ability: to afford at ease the best of all the basic necessities of life. The men of riches feed on the best balanced dietary food and delicacies available; they cannot only afford the best of designer' clothes in the market but also do order for customized clothes that they wear; they live in multi million worth of luxury houses with a paradise-like environment mostly located in the choicest reserved areas in the state.

The men of riches can lavishly afford themselves with the best of every available comfort facilities in life – the best of furniture and furnishings, expensive cars of latest model or in most cases even a private jet, high tech electronics and home appliances of highest quality and performance. The men of riches have the extreme financial ability to acquire, possess and control multiple and chains of valuable financial and material assets and business investments which places them in position as employers of labor up to a minimum of 500 people without any maximum number who are in their payroll working for them to earn a living. They offer the highest level of financial help and support to better and improve on the lives of many individuals and the society at large as much as they may choose to offer.

These men of riches do not engage themselves to do any specific job rather they are owners of highest income yielding multi-diversified organizations or establishments such as conglomerates, corporations, companies, industries or businesses investments and other huge income yielding financial and material assets scattered here and there. Their multi-diversified areas of investments and business operations may including real estate, oil and gas, manufacturing and production, tourism and hospitality, transportation, sports, service delivery, business and trading, exploration and mining, etc. These are usually scattered within their country of residence, across to other countries abroad within their continent, and sometimes to other countries outside their continent. For the men of riches, more or less they own, manager, control, supervise and coordinate the operations of their multi organizations.

With their financial ability they do have a guarantee of highest reserves of savings to take care of any arising accidental expenses and or precautionary emergencies. Unlike the rich, the men of riches are the all-time biggest customers of the banks. The banks do not only offer them most preferential treatment but serve them because they are their richest account holders. They pull the highest financial transactions and business deals with the banks. And for investment purposes, they do have access from the banks to unlimited credit facilities such as huge millions worth of loan, over-drafted funds, partnership contract financing. All these they use either to take advantage of an emerging investment opportunity; to finance to expand the empire of their already existing multi diversified investments or business operations, financial and material assets.

Considering the nature of the territorial size and network of their multi-chains of investments, business operations and assets, the men of riches do often owe the banks but mostly not as much that they can't repay back. Because of their multi investments, business operations and assets, the men of riches are entitled to receiving a geometric inflow of returnable incomes from several sources. These men of riches do make closing balances of their incomes on either daily, weekly or monthly basis obviously because of their hugeness. They can boost of having the financial ability than every other ones to live the highest enhanced quality, affluent and luxury life in the society if they choose to do so. The men of riches do own and possess fleet of latest model of luxury cars in the market. Though that may depend on their individual choices. They make their trips more by air route especially with their own private jets in company of their personal aids.

Also they do have the financial ability to send their children to the highest expensive but best existing schools where they can acquire the highest and the best available quality education. The financial ability of the men of riches do place them in the highest position than anyone else where they have the potential to continue to create and expand their financial wealth. These men of riches are the key players in the private sector of every nation. Apart from the government, the men of riches are the next employer of labor among whom are the paupers, the poor and the rich-poor who work for them while, they sit back to make their get-richer money. As paraphrased, the men of riches are the few lenders who rules over the paupers, the poor and poor-rich who are always their borrowers or dependents *(Prb.22v7)*.

The men of riches do have on their payroll some experts whom they employ to render professional services to them such as doctor, lawyer, accountant, high-tech secretary, etc. In some cases the contractual engagement of these professionals may require them to privately extend their services also to the immediate family members of their boss. Just like the rich, the men of riches also they do have maid servants and other auxiliary house workers who render services to them such as drivers, cooks, gardeners, security men, cleaners, barbers, etc. The men of riches do wield and command power and influence especially throughout their country of resident, in and across other countries.

Just as most of the rich people, the men of riches are directly or indirectly not merely into states politics, but national politics. They do have a good number of political friends and loyalists, sometimes political candidates whom they sponsor for various political offices. They do have and maintain the highest network of connection and contact profile in the society. Their most preferred language to speak is the language of money, investment and income returns. No one communicates with them fluently who does not know how to speak the same language of money, investment and income. The men of riches may not be the commander-in-chief of their nation's armed forces but on the other hand they are the commander-in-chief and controller-in-chief of some of the strategic sectors of their nation's economy.

Their financial wealth have earned them the prestigious award of either state or national consultant on economy especially in their respective state or nation's front. They are always consulted on key issues of government's strategic policy decision, reform or revolution on the economy. Indeed they are the pillars of the economic system. The men of riches are the capitalist lords and bourgeoisies, captains of industries and mogul businessmen who determine the nation's exchange flow and direction. Among these men of riches include: Bill Gates of America, Carlos Slim Helu of Mexico, Liliane Bettencourt of France, Amancio Ortega of Spain, Jeff Bezos of America, etc.

CHAPTER TEN

CHOICES OF FINANCIAL BEHAVIOUR AND DECISION

Owners of money assets

Unfortunately, in the world that is filled with money assets to become rich and to create financial wealth, the poor by their choice of financial behavior have continued to allow the rich to have the advantage of being the owners, possessors and controllers of money assets. To support this fact, a great man once said, *"If you take all the monies in the world and distribute them equally among its people, after a while all the monies will go back to their original owners"*. Who are these owners here referred? The rich of course. Why? It is because of the poor's choice of financial behavior and decision. Their choices of financial behavior is continually leading them to 'Pass Over Opportunities Repeatedly'. In other words their choices of financial behavior is leading them to remain always poor in life.

By their choice of financial behavior, the poor opt out of opportunities to become owners, possessors and controllers of money assets; rather they opt in for perpetual poverty. They seem to only see challenges in every investment opportunity that offers itself, instead of seeing an investment opportunity in every challenge that comes their way. The poor choose to value wages which they prefer to tirelessly work for all through their life. Unlike the rich that choose to value profit which they strategically work for through investment. Obviously, the decision to become rich is hard. But the decision to remain poor is harder.

Why poor people always remain poor

Poor people once they get money, they begin to spend them on daily consumption, sometimes to purchase liabilities in the name of acquiring material property or personal assets, and most often for solving their immediate personal problems until the money is finished; but rich people choose to double whatever money they get through investment before they first spend them. By this choice of financial behavior and decision, the poor spends up their money income just as they receive them, so they remain perpetually poor; but the rich get richer by creating a new source of profits through investment which guarantees a steady inflow of streams of money income. The rich choose to multiply their income; but the poor choose to subtract from their income. You may sometimes need to put your problem on hold and multiply your income first.

Poor people think that with a paid job they could become rich, but rich people knows that only investment could make them become richer. The poor choose to be consumers while the rich choose to be investors.

Poor people avoids taking risk because of their fear of business failure or money loss; but rich people know that if they don't take risk, they have already failed to make more money.

Poor people blame their problems for letting go an investment opportunity to become rich; but rich people swiftly take advantage of any investment opportunity that comes despite their problems.

Poor people prepare and hope for today's money income only; but rich people prepare and hope for today's money income and for tomorrow's income returns.

Poor people depreciates their income prospects by wasting their valuable time on non-value adding things; but rich people do usefully engage and deploy their valuable time as an investment assets for making money.

Poor people wants to reap if possible before they sow their seed of investment, they want to reap the returns the same day without working hard to grow their investment; but rich people takes time to work real hard to grow their investment and wouldn't mind to be patient for long before beginning to reap in folds the returns on their investment.

Poor people do live ignorantly in the world without

knowledge of existing investment opportunities around them, even when they see and are aware of existing investment opportunities; they do lack the interest and motivation to take advantage of them after which they would regret at last; they fear to take risk, they give excuses, and sometimes subject themselves to over analysis for which reason they do prefer to have their money either in their pocket or at bank: What a great mistake! A source is never a channel. Your income is your source, but the money at hand or in the bank account is your channel. So, if you want to have more either at hand or in your bank, then raise the value of your source; the poor believe in the viability of the investment opportunities but choose to take no action except they see others succeed. Unlike the poor people, the rich people seem to search, spot and become aware of exciting investment opportunities; with interest and motivation they take immediate action to size such opportunities without waiting for others to succeed first before them.

Tell the poor about an existing investment opportunity, they think it's a trap. Tell the poor to invest just a little, they will say they can't earn much from it. Tell the poor to make a big time investment, they will say they don't have any money. Tell them to try beginning with new things entirely, they will say they have no experience, and would demand to know if it had worked for others, and to know who had gained from it before. Tell the poor to try an odd business, they will say it is unappealing for them to do. Tell the poor to run a shop, they will say it would tie them down to deny them freedom. The poor do take their unhealthy financial decisions based on the counsel, opinion and advice from their fellow poor people. The poor think like a university professor to be penny wise, but like a blind man they do pound foolish. The poor dwell comfortably within the territory of their knowledge, and anything beyond their reason is considered fraudulent and can't work.

Your decision to find money, is your decision to earn money

If you find money where it is, you can earn money from where it is. According a South African network marketing guru, there are basically three places where money is, and could be found. Of course, no embargo is placed on who should find money where it is. Money is meant to be found by whoever that cares, whether you are already rich or poor. The three places where you will always find money are: with the People; to Find solution; and with Opportunities. If you don't decide to find where money is, you can't earn money in life. Let me explain how you can find money and earn money from these three places.

With the people: No one anywhere in the world who

wouldn't need people to earn money. As soon as you find where money is, you begin to earn money. Ask doctors, they will tell you that they need patients to earn money. Ask lawyers, they will tell you that they need clients to earn money. Ask mortuary attendants and casket makers, they will tell you that they need dead people to earn money. Ask bankers and businessmen, they will tell you that they need customers to earn money. Ask transporters, they will tell you that they need passengers to earn money. Ask pastors or priests, they will tell you that they need worshipping members to earn money. Ask lecturers and teachers, they will tell you that they need students to earn money. Ask mechanics and car technicians, they will tell you that they need drivers and car owners to earn money. Ask footballers, they will tell you that they need fans to earn money. Ask comedians, they will tell you that they need audience to earn money.

Never should you run away from people. You need people from whom to earn money to create financial wealth for you to become rich. Unfortunately, there is a financial system status-quo created by the mechanism of capitalism advantage that has continued to offer the poor as the people that the rich need to continually earn money. What do I mean; a system that has made the rich to become hookers to whom the poor are financial baits for creating more financial wealth for them to become wealthier. Still it is you who must decide to break yourself away from this poverty prone vicious system. You can reverse the system if you choose or decide, either by finding a solution to a need; or by snatching away opportunities before the rich could grab them to their monopoly.

Find a solution to a need: Truly, human wants are unlimited, but human needs are ever emerging to require solution for a complete satisfaction. Money is ever abundantly residing with people who have needs. Locate these people and find solution to their needs, then you will begin to earn money from them. They are willing to pay for any solution to their need, even at a higher price for your higher earning. This is one of the ways to change the status quo of being the people that the rich need to earn money. Instead, make several others to become the people that you can offer solution to their needs and start earning money big time from them.

Sometimes finding a solution to your own problems can open doors for you to sale your solution to earn money from other people who may be facing similar problems. So, don't always choose or decide to run away from your problems. Finding a solution to them could become a stepping stone for you to start earning money to create financial wealth. Ask those who have created financial wealth, they will tell you of a need or certain need of people that they found solution to. You too can join them and create your own financial wealth too. The possibility begins with your choice.

With opportunities: At every time, in everywhere, and in every condition of human living, there are always opportunities that offer themselves up for one to make investment in order to create financial wealth. The creators of financial wealth see these opportunities as rare ones for investment from which they can earn future returns. They never see these investment opportunities and let them pass over them. At sight they analyze them, go for them and quickly grab them ahead of possible competition. The financial wealth creators focus more on the level of future returns that an investment opportunity would offer them, and not necessarily on the nature of it or where it is coming from.

Unfortunately, it is more pitiful that sometimes most of these investment opportunities are even created by the poor people through their choice of financial behavior and decision. What a financial irony that favors the rich against the poor. Investment opportunities have always existed in every generation of human history. That's why in every past generation there were records of men who took advantage of investment opportunities and succeed in creating financial wealth. Even from the Biblical accounts, we have Abraham, Isaac, Jacob, David, Solomon, and Job, etc. These were men who at their respective time and in their respective measure were able to create generational financial wealth because they did take advantage of available investment opportunities.

You may ask, where and what are the sources of investment opportunities? Investment opportunities are offered by the yearly times and seasons; state or condition of human living which determines human needs; information and knowledge; forces of the capitalist prices; government programs – policies, decisions and decrees; periods of economic phases – inflation, recession, recovery, and boom; and people's choices of financial behavior and decision. At least if you are not positioned with the financial means to take advantage of an investment opportunity that either of these sources offer; then be sure that you don't create opportunity for the rich to be richer through your choice of financial behavior and decision. Otherwise you will get poorer while the rich get richer. For as soon as you create any opportunity by your financial behavior and decision, the rich will quickly spot them and pounce on them. Because the rich are opportunity hunters. Of course, they choose to do their hunting at the jungle forest of the poor. Your choice of financial behavior and decision alone can open the poverty-prison gate for you to escape, only if you choose to.

Jeff Bezos, one of the great men of riches, who owns

Amazon Company was one of such men that took advantage of an investment opportunity that information and his knowledge as a computer scientist offered. In 1994, Jeff Bezos read that the web had grown 2,300% in one year. This number astounded him, and he decided he needed to find some way to take advantage of its rapid growth. He made a list of 20 possible products to sell online and decided books were the best option. Hence, Bezos launched out Amazon which went public on May 15, 1997. And today, Amazon's capitalization is worth more than $500 billion besides several other investments, assets and property. What a massive creation of financial wealth that is worth more than riches!

With forfeiture of self-gratification: Another great place that is unknown to many where you can actually find huge amount of money to invest for wealth creation, is in your forfeiture of immediate self-gratification. You must be cautious of not spending much of the money you have today only on things that would gratify you at moment. To spend money for self-gratification simply means to acquire things that mostly could give you immediate comfort, pleasure, mere satisfaction and or self-pride. Examples of such things include: expensive and exotic building or house, cars, phones, electronics, clothes and shoes, wrist watches and necklace, holiday trips, house parties or celebrations, etc. You are invariably eating up your today's investment and your future financial wealth when you allow yourself become so addicted to spending excessive money for your immediate gratification.

Oh yes, during the early years of my ministry, I remembered I had to forfeit what I considered to be immediate self-gratification. I had to live in my apartment that was not furnished even with the most common electronic appliances; I never got myself the best of clothes and shoes, I equally did minimize my expenses for personal consumptions, not because I couldn't afford them as at then. But because at that moment I needed to take up an investment project worth thousands of dollars that I knew would help to enhance my effectiveness and performance in the work of the ministry for an upgrade of my career value and earning worth as well as to bring in more money income to me in the long run. Eventually I ended up finding and earning the amount of thousands of dollars that I needed for the investment project all from the forfeiture of my immediate self-gratification. In the long run the investment project proved worthwhile and successfully resulted to a better inflow of income, higher savings, and more opportunity for me to continue to invest to create more financial wealth which is useful to me for the financing God's work.

In fact, every penny in your hand especially now that you are young is like a seed. It is your choice to decide either to eat it up or to sow it into the fertile ground of investment. And be assured that in the nearest future you will begin to reap its returns in higher fold. Addiction to spending money for self-gratification leads to poverty. The opportunity cost of the money you forfeited for your self-gratification is the investment you will have made for yourself by the same money. Forfeiture of expenditure for self-gratification is your personal rich bank where you can borrow money to make a lasting investment from which you would be earning residual income.

There is a typical story of two young men from down town Nigeria in Africa with the names; Shina Peters and Jim Ovia, both of whom once had the same equal amount of money to create a generational financial wealth. Of course, by forfeiture of his immediate self-gratification, Jim Ovia did found the initial money that he needed to invest to establish what has today become one of the most financially viable, stable, and performing bank in Nigeria and beyond. And today he has succeeded in building a generational financial wealth. But unlike him, Shina Peters couldn't forfeit his immediate self-gratification. By this unfortunate choice he lost the initial money he could have invested to create a generational financial wealth to a mere house which today is standing as a liability that still requires more money for its maintenance with no yield of returns. Let's go through their stories in details.

In 1990, Shina Peters lavishly built a house with a whopping amount of NGN 20 million naira. The same year Jim Ovia started Zenith Bank with the same amount. Today people in Nigeria except for Shina Peters' family members, do not have a room in his house, but a mammoth number of Nigerians do have an account with Zenith bank. Shina Peters' house was built in the metropolitan city of Lagos where it still stands dilapidating every year. But Jim's bank started just in a corner but today has over 500 branches in Nigeria alone besides her many international branches with millions of daily transactions taking place.

In 2015, Shina Peters spent additional millions of money to renovate his multi-million house and then bought a Nissan Pathfinder worth NGN 10 million naira. That's an additional liability, where as in the same year Jim's bank made staggering profit of NGN 105.7 billion naira. Today Zenith bank employs hundreds of thousands of people who feed their families. Jim Ovia is today worth over $980 million dollars just with a startup of an investment of NGN 20 million

With Your Assets and Property or Business Investment: The assets or property or business investment that you owe is also one other place where you can find money to alternatively make a new investment that could be fetching you more earnings of money. Your immediate financial potential to begin to earn more money lies in the assets or property or business investment that are yours already. However, being ignorant of your financial potentials would always limit your chances of creating more financial wealth in life.

Among the poor, it is unfortunate that many of them are owners of either depreciating assets and property or outdated business investment, yet they are still poor. Simply because they are yet to understand that there are money in the place of their assets and property or business investment. These assets or property may include: Savings or Fixed bank deposit; Landed Property: plots of land and buildings; Automobile or Vehicles; Bonds, shares and or Debentures; intellectual property, etc. While business investment may include: exploration and extractive; processing; manufacturing or production; farming or animal rearing; service and consultancy; entertainment and sports; trading and merchandizing company, corporation, or conglomerate.

There is what I call, "the law of transfer to an alternative new business investment". I consider this a great law of financial management of assets and property or business investment. Every already owned asset or property or existing business investment that you have has what I call both its "Money worth" and "Earning worth". Money worth is the 'current market value' which is the amount of money that your asset or property could be sold at the current given time. While earning worth is the 'future financial value' which is the amount of income returns that your already owned asset or property or existing business investment could be yielding in future if sold at present and transferred to an alternative new business investment of either a short, medium or long time-span.

Because every already asset or property owned or existing business investment has a money worth, therefore such can be transferred to an alternative new business investment. Especially if their current income yielding performance rate is low or getting fast lower. However, this law of transfer to an alternative new business investment states that, *"your asset or property or already existing business investment can be transferred to an alternative new business investment that has potential for a higher future earning worth within a considerable time span than its present money worth compared"*.

For instance, assuming you have an empty plot of land that has a money worth of $50,000 toady; but would in next three years appreciate to a money worth of $70,000. And perhaps as at today you come across an opportunity to invest $50,000 to a new line of business investment that has a viable financial prospect of yielding an earning worth of $100,000 within the time-span of the same three years. In this case, the earning worth of the new line of business investment is evidently higher than the money worth of your current owned asset, property or business investment.

Within the same time-span of three years, the money worth of your asset or property would bring to you a financial gain of $20,000 only.

While the earning worth of the new line of business investment would bring to you a higher financial gain of $50,000. Then comparing the two financial gains, it only would make sense that you give up such an asset or property or already business investment for sale at its money worth (current market value) and then transfer it to an alternative new line of business investment that would bring higher earning worth for you. This law you must be ready to apply whenever necessary if at all you must create more financial wealth in life.

Let's consider the case of *Lee Byung-Chull*, the owner of Samsung Company, how he has continued to increase his earning worth by applying the law of transfer to an alternative business investment.

In 1938, Lee Byung-chull launched Samsung in South Korea as a grocery shop. In 1940, due to tight competition in the grocery business sector, Samsung alternatively transferred his business investment from grocery to production and selling of noodles. In 1950, Samsung alternatively transferred his business investment from noodles to production of sugar. In 1954, Samsung alternatively transferred his business investment from sugar to woolen mill business. In 1956, Samsung alternatively transferred his business investment from woolen mill to Insurance and Securities selling business. In 1960, Samsung alternatively transferred his business investment from insurance and securities to manufacturing of Television – the black and white brand. In 1980, Samsung alternatively transferred his business investment from television to Telecoms business, producing telephone switch boards.

In 1987, Lee Byun-Chull, the founder of Samsung died. Then the company split into four independent subsidiary companies – Department stores; Chemicals and logistics; Paper and Telecom; and Electronics. In the same year Samsung Company now managed by Lee's son as the new CEO decided to focus on international investment of plants and semi-conductor facilities around the world. In 1990, Samsung alternatively transferred his business investment from semi-conductors to build the world's tallest towers – Petronas Towers Malaysia, and Taipei 101 in Taiwan. In 1993 when the Asian market went belly up because of heavy recession, Samsung alternatively downsized his business investment; sold parts of his subsidiary companies; and then merged the rest of Electronics, Engineering and Chemicals together. By this merger, Samsung became the world's largest producer of memory chips.

In 1995, Samsung alternatively transferred his business investment from memory chip production to Liquid-crystal displays, and for 10 years he became the world's largest manufacturer of Flat Screen Television. In 2010, with liquid crystal display becoming competitive, Samsung launches a 10 year growth strategy, with manufacturing of smart phones being a key focus. And just in 2016, Samsung became the world's largest Mobile and Smart Phone manufacturer, outselling iPhone at the ratio of two to one. As at the year 2017, Samsung's sales is over $250 billion, and produces a fifth of South Korea's total export.

Therefore don't be afraid of embarking or embracing change if you must boast of higher earnings than money worth. For if you don't go for change or move along with it, you may only have money but not financial wealth. Don't get stuck doing same thing continuously. Delve into new waters. Creating financial wealth is in the new not in the old same thing. Take the risk to explore and take advantage of the new.

CHAPTER ELEVEN

REQUIREMENTS FOR CREATING FINANCIAL WEALTH

Rules for creating financial wealth

The art-craft of creating financial wealth requires seven fundamental rules as follows:

1. No shortcuts anywhere to follow that will get you out of poverty. It requires an art-craft process to create financial wealth for you to get out of poverty.
2. No quick fixes of your past poverty-caused financial mistakes, failures, and lost opportunities; lest you may fail to learn your lessons and stumble again at their repeat.
3. No blaming of others for your past financial mistakes, failures or lost opportunities; lest you may lack the motivation and drive to create financial wealth.
4. Never say no, not today, I will do it tomorrow – that's procrastination. Else you may fall victim to your own waiting, perhaps for a perfect time or right moment that may never come; for you to be appointed or promoted which may not happen; for you to be ready or prepared better which may

not be a reality soonest; for you to be favored by powers that be which may not be granted. There is never any sudden moment when everything makes perfect sense and the road to creating financial wealth becomes effortless.

5. Start at the age 0 – 30 to prepare yourself for the vision of creating financial wealth by training yourself to acquire every necessary knowledge and by learning to gain every skills required to engage yourself with a career job at this stage of life.

6. Start working hard at the age of 31- 50 to earn money income from a career job and make sustainable investments for future inflow of returnable incomes that would guarantee you a settled, successful and happy retirement from the age of 51 – and above.

If you don't work hard at your youthful age to successfully creating financial wealth, you will spend the rest of your old age being a miserable dependent poor father or mother. If you live your youthful life taking wrong financial decision to disobey the above rules for creating financial wealth; it will lead you to an adulthood of financial struggles which will take you to an old age of financial regrets and poverty. Therefore, do all you can at your earning stage in life to give your future generation an inheritance of financial wealth that will open for them the doors of influence and power in life which they do deserve. For if you are born poor, it's not your fault; but if you die poor or raise poor children, then it's your fault and a curse for your children.

Positive financial mindset

To have a positive financial mindset is to set your mind on the truth that you can become rich in life by creating financial wealth for yourself. Having a positive mindset is to accept and believe the truth that you are created to be rich and not to be poor in life.

Men with negative financial mindset do believe in Satan's lies and deception that they cannot become rich in life. They mostly live with the wrong idea or belief that they don't have at all what it takes to become rich – a job to do, well paid job for that matter, rich parents, connections, academic qualifications, and money even. For such men, they do always think in error that certain individuals than some others are created and only destined to become rich. While some others are unfortunately not, however it is not true.

On the other side, men with pro-financial mind-set do believe in the possibility of them becoming rich. They do believe that they can soar higher into the great altitude of creating higher measure of financial wealth than they are experiencing presently. It is only a pro-financial mindset that can leave you with an unquenchable hunger to create financial wealth in life. Therefore beware, for Eagles fly alone and to high altitudes: Stay away from narrow minded people; those that bring you down with their negative mindset about creating financial wealth. An eagle flies with eagles. Keep good company of people of the same like mind. Don't waste time with people who don't have the positive mindset that it is possible to create financial wealth, even from the mud of poverty.

Someone says, *"It takes the mind to see great opportunities, not the eyes"*. And only those with positive mindset can see around them such opportunities for creating financial wealth. Poverty is a product of mindset for it actually begins from the mind. No matter your much effort, living with a negative mindset will never give you a positive life. The limit is not in the sky, it is in the mind. Becoming an owner and possessor of financial wealth is possible but only for those who have made up their mind not to give up, not to give in and not to throw in the trowel even when their mind is negatively saying otherwise.

It is only a man with a pro-financial mindset who would dare not to leave any stone unturned, not until he evacuates himself from the ugly refugee camp of financial failure and poverty in life. If you don't develop a pro-financial mindset you might not be able to rise up to the challenging task of being inspired by the idea of the fact that you are God's wonderful creature destined to create financial wealth and to live to enjoy riches. You can't afford at any price whatsoever to take chances of living and ending your life here on earth in poverty, knowing that poverty won't have any place in heaven should you by God's grace make eternity into heaven. As a believer, that you have a hope of eternity into heaven where you shall certainly live in the transcending riches of God's financial wealth shouldn't be the reason why you would choose to be poor while on earth.

Put your past financial mistakes behind

Failures or limitations of the past have no control over the greatness in you. The present is the reality moment between the past and the future. Of course, the present after all is the only moment that is one's real time. *"Nothing is as far as one hour ago"- John Mason*. Since it is not possible that you could recall back the past of your life, you must learn to let it go just as Paul did *(Ph.3v13)*. Listen to the wisdom of *Carl Bard*, *"Though no one can get back and make a brand new start, but anyone can start from now and make a brand new ending"*. Past is often destructive and could obstruct our lives. Past is a life vicissitude that we should deal with if we must achieve greatness in life. The truth is that the past does not equal the future. Because you failed all through yesterday or even today, or a moment ago does not really matter. All that matters is, what are you doing or gonna do right now? Therefore, ignore the negative voice of your past financial mistakes that may be speaking to your head.

Past is a waste paper to be used no more, present is a newspaper still to be read, and future is a question paper to be answered. Come out of your past, control the present, and secure the future. You can either let your past to define you, destroy you or strengthen you. The choice is for you to make. We use pencil when we were a child, but now that we are adult we use pen. Do you know why? Because mistakes in childhood of our past can easily be erased now in the adulthood of our present. You must learn to put behind all the memories and ugly experiences of your past financial mistakes – wrong investment made, investment opportunity lost, irrecoverable bad debt, decision to avoid risk, extravagant spending, ignorance and or negligence of financial principles that did get you into financial poverty or hardship. Past financial mistakes put together could either be a mismanagement or misappropriation of one's money income during one's yesterday.

"Life is too precious and too short to sit around regretting lost opportunities. Get up and get going"- Anonymous. "Even a mistake may turn out to be one thing necessary to a wonderful achievement"- Henry Ford. As a way of putting your past ugly experiences and memories of financial mistakes behind, you should begin to detect and lay hold to the new financial

opportunities that the present and the future hold for you. No matter how much you try, you cannot create a settled financial future for yourself if you don't learn to use financial prospects that the present holds for you to crash out your ugly pass records of financial mistakes that kept you in poverty. In spite of your past financial mistakes, bless yourself and say it is well with me. Why? Because you can still rise all the way to change that past story.

With the experiences of your past financial mistakes which may have landed you into poverty, learn to be financially forward-obsessed and not backward-obsessed. The more you borrow from the past memories of your financial mistakes, the more you will continue to incur the debt of more financial despair. But the more you begin to lend hope to your today, the more tomorrow will begin to yield to you an interest of a better financial world. Don't condemn yourself for your past financial mistakes - fumbles, messes, ignorance or negligence that got you arrested by the hands of financial poverty. These may include your choice in the past to be idle; your wasteful and extravagant spending on non-basic things – like ceremonies; your past competitive spending for mere ego and pride; your over borrowing beyond your income; your wrong and unguided investment or assets acquisition; your excessive free lending to others based on sympathy; negligence and procrastinated response to an existed or emerged financial opportunity.

You see, concerning the issue of mistakes, we all have made mistakes; we all still makes mistakes; and we are still gonna make mistakes. But hear this after all, *"if silly things were not done, intelligent things would never happen"- Tom Peters. "A big man is not one who makes no mistakes, but one who is bigger than any mistake he makes"- Zig Ziglar. "No matter how many mistakes you make or how slow you progress, you are still way ahead of everyone who isn't trying" – Tony Robins. The* greatest men of riches in the anal of history have never lived without some rugged-dirty-slates of past financial mistakes. They learnt their lessons from their financial mistakes. And all they did was to set ablaze to ashes their past files full of odd memories of their financial mistakes; after which they opened up for themselves new files of an inspiring right choice that gave them the rising confidence to have made self-speaking landmark of financial breakthroughs and creation of financial wealth. You too can do the same. Your past financial success is only a small inking of what the future holds.

Eagles do not eat Dead things. They feed only on fresh prey: Do not rely on your past successes; keep looking for new frontiers to conquer. Leave your past where it belongs, in the past. The courtyard of past is a nice place to visit but certainly not a good place to stay. Only your tomorrow can offer a better life for you, not your yesterday. Do not relish on yesterday's success. Achievement is a continuous process; keep the fire burning always.

Make it your choice to create financial wealth

However, it is important for you to note that whatever measure of financial wealth as a dimension of prosperity that God has created you to achieve is sealed with the eternal blood of the Lamb and made certain by the Word of God. It is now therefore at your discretion to make it your choice either to achieve this dimension of prosperity in life or not. If you dare fail to make it your choice to create financial wealth, it means you have accepted the fate to live all through in poverty.

Remember, the four lepers at the entrance gate of Samaria made the right choice to break the bond of poverty off their lives and stepped into financial survival that made them rose up and walked out of begging. They believed in themselves, put behind them their past mistakes, remained committed to their choice to explore the risky opportunity to secure their financial survival out of poverty. All these they were able to do for themselves not in too long a time. And with it they were able to set on motion the wheel of their life that finally took them to a destination of glory instead of mediocrity. You too can equally make it your choice to create financial wealth. I bet you, just try it and you too will get there.

CHAPTER TWELVE

PRINCIPLES FOR CREATING FINANCIAL WEALTH 1

Principle of engaging yourself to do a career job

Remember that one of your destiny contents is your intention to pursue a career dream. This never becomes a reality until you translate it into the act of engaging yourself to do a particular career job that best fits with the career dream you had intended to pursue in life. Once you have engaged yourself into a career job, you are sure that you are on the path way to creating financial wealth for yourself. It is only when you have started creating financial wealth that you can be sure to live a rich life with a greater financial ability to be able, to take care of your basic personal needs, to provide for your family and educate your children, to positively impact on people's lives, society, and your generation. In fact, without actively and productively engaging yourself to do a career job for you to earn income, you may not be able to create financial wealth let alone to achieve other dimensions of prosperity.

Of course, the big question is, what is a career job for a source of income and how do I begin with it? Simply put it, *"a career job is that particular dream job or occupation of choice that you have actively and productively engaged yourself to do from which you earn income to create financial wealth".*

"Then God…, rested from all His work…, For we are His workmanship, created in Christ Jesus for good works…, Prepared for every good work (Gen.2v3, Eph.2v10, 2Tim.2v21).

Evidently, God has been and is still the master workman. For six days, He worked to create and make all things. He still works even now. And you are a product of His craftwork. That's why you are His workmanship created in Christ Jesus but prepared by destiny to be able to do a work too. God cannot be the creator-worker and creates one who would not be a worker also. After God's creation of man, the first thing He did was to put man to work at the Garden of Eden. So, God had created you to be a worker and a laborer who after working would deserve your wage as income. Of course, having a career job that you do is actually the starting point for anyone who wants to create financial wealth and migrate out of poverty in life.

The question often asked is, how can a career dream that one intends to pursue in life be translated into a career job that one could engage oneself to do as a source of income? It is simple. For instance, the career dream that you are intending to pursue in life may be either to become a musician, an actor, a clergy, a lawyer, a doctor, a teacher, a builder, a transporter, an office clerk, a businessman or woman, an auto mechanic, a car washer, a plumber, a fruit seller, a vendor, a civil or a public servant etc. Yes, becoming either of the above can guarantee you a source of income by which you can create financial wealth.

However, every career dream you choose to pursue in life has a career job that it translates into, of which you can actively and productively engage yourself into; especially if you have adequately acquired and equipped yourself either with the required academic training and knowledge or apprenticeship training and job experience. That is to say for instance, if your career dream is to become a doctor, then you must be prepared to acquire every necessary training and learning or knowledge and experience required for its professional practice.

Why at all do you need to begin with a career job, you may want to know? It is because you can't create financial wealth out of nothing but through something that you do from which you are earning income. Creating financial wealth is not by begging but by beginning to do something that is exchangeable in value for money no matter how little it might be. You also can't create financial wealth by stealing but by starting with something doable. Neither can you create financial wealth by only faith with prayer without work, but by paying the price of working hard to earn income. Financial wealth as a dimension of prosperity is not created by mere wishing but by mean-working. Obviously you must have a career job that you do or an occupation that you engage yourself into as your means of earning income whether as paid employment, business or trading, self-empowered employment, skill or craft handiwork, menial work, or as a professional career practitioner, etc.

Then whatever career job that you choose to engage yourself into must be a reflection of your career dream. If not, one may for long in life be struggling to create financial wealth. You can't be idle doing nothing and expect to create financial wealth. Hear this, never should you allow your life as a field to overgrow to be covered with fallow of idleness. For *"He who (have something doing) tills his land will have plenty of bread (money), but he who follows frivolity (idleness) will have poverty enough" (Prb.28v19)*. Otherwise if you do, it means you are yet to have the understanding of how you can begin to create financial wealth.

The wise man Solomon puts it better this way, *"I went by the field of the lazy man, and by the vineyard of the man devoid of understanding; and there it was, all overgrown with thorns; ... covered with nettles; ... when I saw it, I considered it well; I looked at it and received instruction: A little sleep, a little slumber, a little folding of hands to rest; so shall your poverty come like a prowler, and your need like an armed man" (Prb.24v30-34)*. Engaging yourself to do a particular career job is what separates you from financial poverty. A source-of-income career job requires that you give out something of value in exchange in order to earn either an instant, daily or periodic income. Without engaging yourself to do a career job, you will face limitation in creating financial wealth. An idle man will never create financial wealth let alone to live a rich life, no matter how great his destiny may be.

Now that you have understood that you need to begin with a career job that will be a source of income to you. The obvious challenging question has always been; how would you know the exact career job or occupation God wants you to do that is actually connected to your destiny? Consequently, such questions as the following do often arise. Is it part of God's destiny for me to be a businessman or woman and what kind of business? Is it part of God's destiny for me to be a clergy and into which ministry; is it on full or part time basis? Is it part of God's destiny for me to be a graduate and what course should I study? Is it part of God's destiny for me to be a professional and what area of professional career job, say to be a doctor, lawyer, engineer, etc. No doubt these questions are not always so easy to answer by anyone.

Bill Newman suggested, "If you had anything you wanted – unlimited time, unlimited money, unlimited information, unlimited wisdom, unlimited staff, all the resources you could ask – what would you do? Your answer to this question may not be far from what career job that you should be doing to earn income –

usually a reflection of your career dream. However in most cases, you may be inspired and motivated to know the particular career job or occupation that God wants you to do mainly by revelations either through an inspired inner insight of ideas or thoughts, other people's achievement, personal yearning and interest, advice or testimonies of others, experience or circumstance, events and or incidents in people's life.

Nevertheless, it is often not easy in life to discover or know the exact career job or occupation that God wants you to do. If you do choose a career job or occupation that is not connected to your destiny, you may find yourself struggling to build financial success through it. The truth is that once your chosen career job or occupation is connected to your destiny, whatever you do whether a street fruit seller or truck pusher, you can through it make a financial survival to become rich. That is exactly how it works. Of course, your chosen or preferred career job or occupation must not be disapproved by the scriptures or be a vice against the society.

Let me explain further with biblical examples. Joseph in *Gen.37* pictured the career dream of his destiny to become a national leader and political administrator which eventually became his career job for a source of income. With the career job he was able to create for himself an amazing financial wealth that his family later benefited from. Moses too caught the career dream of his destiny to become a great Deliverer, Leader and Judge instead of being a royal Astrology and a Magician in Egypt as in *(Gen.2v11-14)*, which eventually became his career job. With the career job he was able to successfully create a lasting financial wealth too.

Also, David's career dream of destiny was to become a King-Leader, a champion Deliverer and a Great Judge over Israel *(1Sam.17v34-36)*, which eventually became his career job for a source of income through which he successfully built financial wealth. What about Solomon whose career dream of destiny was to become a famous King-Leader of Israel, a Great Judge, a political administrator and diplomat, and philosophical teacher which eventually became his career job for a source of income. With his career job he was able to create exceeding great financial wealth that he became exceedingly great rich. All you need is to begin with a career job from which you can earn income, then you will be pretty sure of stepping out successfully to create financial wealth in life.

A career job as a means of livelihood gives you opportunity to earn income which further provides you with money. While money empowers you to create financial wealth. And financial wealth opens door for you to become rich. It is financial wealth that changes your position and increases your economic worth in life and in the society. Rivers don't struggle to flow, and you will never struggle financially in life, because you deserve to enjoy the best of it. Hold on to a career job so you would be able to earn money needed for you to create financial wealth. And then you will migrate from poverty to riches. Your financial vision to create financial wealth won't die; your plans to actualize it won't fail; God's destiny for you to live to enjoy the prosperity of financial wealth won't be aborted; and the desire of your heart to become a man of riches would turn out a reality. The dreams that come true in life are the ones you chase. If you do nothing, you achieve nothing. Therefore, set a career dream and pursue it to actualize it by engaging yourself to do a career job that your career dream translates into.

Principle of small beginning

One of the great principles of creating financial wealth is to begin small if you can't begin big at the moment. *"The secret of getting ahead is getting started" – Agatha Christie.* No other time than now is better for you to seek for and engage yourself into doing a career job. From the career job you will be entitled to earn a steady flow of income which is required for you to be able to create financial wealth. Creating financial wealth is a life time destiny-fulfilling-project that you must finish. Also, it is a war that you must battle to win *(Luk.14v25-33)*. Though to create financial wealth do often seem to appear more capital intensive. Like I said earlier, you may not even need too much money for you to begin to create financial wealth. But what you actually need is a source of income career job, no matter how small you may begin of it. At the beginning, the career job you choose to engage yourself to do may not be attractive and lucrative, but may be a menial and odd work. Not minding, just begin. Do you know why? Because, *"successful people do what unsuccessful people are not willing to do" – Jeff Olson, the WWC wrestler, the Slight Edge.*

Robert Schuller says, "Inch by Inch, everything is by inch". Never surrender to such forces as poverty – lack of money. Don't allow lack of money to determine when you will begin to create financial wealth. But with a career job from which you are earning money you can actually begin. There is always a way to raise the capital you need. You may have to save and count your pennies through your small earning of income from a career job, but somehow the money will come. There is a universal principle that always manifests itself: Money flows through small beginnings. All you need is to spend enough time, use enough energy, extend human relations, put your best effort and work hard to do your small career job, and money will flow little by little into your hands. *"The moment one definitely commits oneself, then providence moves"- W. N. Muarry.*

No matter how small your beginning may be, the most

important thing is for you to begin to do something that can offer value and earn you income. Job says, *"Though your beginning may be small, yet your latter end would increase abundantly" (Job8v7)*. Meanwhile, you must not allow the lion of laziness and shame that is often outside there to become reasons for you not to begin to do any available small career job. Be warned with this scripture, *"The lazy man says, there is a lion in the road! A fierce lion is in the street! As a door turns on its hinges, the lazy man buries his hand in the bowl; it wearies him to bring it back to his mouth. The lazy man is wiser in his own eyes than seven men who are sensibly" (Prb.26v13-16)*.

Starting life in a new country can be hard, but starting a new life with nothing is much harder. Yet many did start with nothing but today they have made it big time. Yes, financial wealth tends to create more financial wealth, yet a rich background is not the only way to the top. Some of the world's wealthiest people started out all from humble and dirt poor beginning. The richest man in Africa has this to say, *"I built a conglomerate and emerged the richest black man in 2008 but it didn't happen overnight. It took me 30 years to get to where I am today. Youths of today aspire to be like me but they want to achieve it overnight. It's not going to work. To build a successful business, you must start small and dream big, in the journey of entrepreneurship, tenacity of purpose is supreme"* – Aliko Dangote.

Also, there is a man I respect so much; a great achiever and a financial wealth creator, Dr. I. K. Odoh, MD, the

CEO of Meridian Hospital, Port-Harcourt, Nigeria, is one of those men from a poor background who started from a scratch and small beginning. As a young graduate doctor from college, he officially began his private medical practice in 1996, in a small rented apartment. But within a space of 21 years today, he has built a well-equipped state-of-the-art private owned conglomerate hospital of international standard known for its best professional performance and excellence in medical practice in Africa. The hospital complex made up of multiple gigantic buildings equipped with modern medical and clinical equipment, instruments and machines is a standout edifice worth more than half a million dollar in current value.

As a medical consultant, his hospital which hosts a great number of employed and contracted medical personnel is not only a centre for quality medical healthcare delivery services to thousands of patients including the expatriate and non-expatriate staff of oil companies, oil servicing companies and other big incorporated companies who come to access medical treatment and check-ups; but also it is a centre for specialty medical training, research and experiment. Today, Dr. I. K. is a visiting medical consultant to many well-known government hospitals within and abroad especially in UK. Though a medical doctor by profession, yet not only does he has knowledge of financial wealth creation principles and strategies but also he is wealth creation driven through assets acquisition besides investments especially in the medical sector wherein he has continued to create a generational empire of financial wealth.

You too can, no matter how small you may want to begin. So, allow yourself to be a beginner. No one starts at the top. You've got to be a beginner before you can be anything else. Don't be ashamed of beginning little to engage and do that job which is not evil provided it becomes a source of income to you. This would turn out to become useful, enhancive and helpful in facilitating both your effort and commitment to create financial wealth, perhaps in the long run. Because, *"To resist at the beginning is always the easiest choice to make, but it's also the only choice that guarantees you will never reach the end result you desire for" – Anonymous.*

Principle of career excellence

An Indian adage says, *"Pursue excellence, and success will chase you, pants down".* It is neither a 100% hard-work, knowledge, leadership, opportunity nor money that makes your life 100% successful, but a 100% attitude of excellence towards life and work, is what does. You will successfully become much closer to creating financial wealth, only if you could perhaps build an attitude of excellence towards life and your job or business.

According to *John Hope Bryant, CEO of Operation Hope*, "*Excellence is a choice. You will never 'drift' into excellence and greatness. And no one else can deliver you into …*" In fact, excellence is an attitude you cultivate, while greatness is a destination you select.

Excellence in career is a very expensive gift. You expect it only from people who becomes great in life. They also have it to offer as a principle for creating financial wealth to survive financial poverty. Don't waste your time playing away your productive time, invest your limited time on training yourself to build career excellence that would make you live your dreamed life in future. Never design your life like a garden where anyone can walk in and out. Design it like the sky where everyone aspires to reach.

A man from Nigeria, by name *John Momoh* once lived in a one-room apartment with 7 of his siblings and parents. They were poor. Young John had to hawk things to make ends meet. Years later, he was one of the best newscasters in the Nigerian Television Authority (NTA) when he quitted his job to pursue what seemed like a 'crazy' dream: to start a privately owned news and current affairs TV station. Today after years of surmounting mountains of challenges, striving for excellence and actually working hard in excellence, CHANNELS TV has reached the very top in Nigeria's TV industry. His life teaches us that success always comes when you constantly strive for

EXCELLENCE in service. The career excellence he built had enabled him to not only create financial wealth; live a rich life but also to become an employer of labor.

Whatever is your choice of career job, it is important that you set for yourself a goal to achieve career excellence. Career excellence is the marketable value (knowledge, skill, experience, expertise, performance) of your career competence that gives you advantage over other competitors in the field of your career job. Career excellence is what defines employee's professionalism, productivity, and profitability value to his employer. Your career excellence becomes for you the lifeline ticket to exceed others in professional performance and to edge others out in career competition. In the field of your career job, it is your career excellence that separates and distinguishes you from your fellow colleagues. Your career excellence is your branded niche for which you are known among others. Career excellence requires that you carve out for yourself a specialized hybrid way of performing your career job better than others.

Career excellence is all about building a proving trademark of positive niche-values and high result-oriented performance in your career job that gives you a higher net wage value. It is career excellence that makes you to become highly sought after within the territory of your career job. Endeavor to increase your niche-values and performance ability to build an attractive and high valued career excellence by learning personal and ethical discipline; acquiring career knowledge; professionalism and expertise through formal training; vocational couching; seminars, conferences and workshops. To earn more from your career job you must seek to acquire additional relevant skills and knowledge that could enhance your ability to serve and perform better. Of course, integrity and honesty are the core niche-values of career excellence. If you choose to be corrupt in your career, you will only have a price; but if you choose integrity and honesty, you will have a value. Both may actually not get you a lot of friends but they will always get you to the right people who knows the worth of your career excellence.

Every employer and hirer of labor whether government, private organizations, captains of industries, and or mogul businessmen is all looking out for employees and workers that have track record and profile of career excellence. What it would only cost you to be on their payroll is to have a built profile of career excellence. The more you are building career excellence, the more you are placing higher value on yourself that would make you more attractive to big time employers of labor. In fact, the higher your profile of career excellence, the higher you will be in demand in the labor market. Career excellence not academic certificates is the core factor that determines the price and reward of labor whether as a wage or salary.

Career excellence can be built by the way of: moral conscience and discipline for value concept, academic training for self-development, career job training and learning for skills to perform better, and career job practice for mastery. Academic training for self-development has to do with you attending an academic institution to acquire and equip yourself with the required intellectual, practical and theoretical self-development knowledge about your choice course of study that is relevant to your career job. The academic institution may be the conventional university, technical or Apprenticeship College, or any other specialized training institutions as the case may be.

Career job training and learning may include attending and participating in trainings, seminars or workshops that are relevant to your career job; and undertaking job-on training or refresher career courses to learn more about your career job for improved performance. Also, career job practice for mastery requires you to continually perform and do your job until you make mastery of it. At this point you can with ease do or perform your career job both effectively and efficiently to the satisfaction of your employer or customers as the case may be.

Until you build up a level of career excellence, you may remain a serving slave to others in your professional career. And without a career excellence, you may remain unemployed even when there is existing employment opportunities or job vacancies. Of course every career job is now professionally competitive. Only those with better career excellence will always survive the labor market competition.

Principle of effective management and efficient usage of capital resource

Capital resources are the take-off resources that you needed in life to begin to create financial wealth so as to live a rich life out of poverty. All men is entitled to have the same equal number of these initial capital resources at his disposal, but a man's judicious management of them determines how financially rich he would become in life more than others. It is better to fail and endure the shame of it than to be a financial failure and stand to face the disgrace and disappointment that goes with it. Come to think of it by the way, are you born to be a financial failure? Not at all, you are neither created nor born to be a financial failure but to be financially successful in life. That is part of why you are here and living too.

You are too destined in life only for you to live in poverty. God has so created you that all through your life you would have access to a certain portion of these initial capital resources. You need nothing else than these initial capital resources as your take-off requirement for creating financial wealth for yourself. With your effective and judicious use of them you can completely move out from the camp of financial failure. These initial capital resources are: **Time, Brain** and **Talent**.

In order to enable you and I to be able to create financial wealth as a dimension of prosperity, by the eternal capacity of God's magnanimity He has graciously provided us with the same equal initial capital resources of: valuable **time** of 24hours 7 at our disposal; electrifying creative **brain** both to generate new seed of financial wealth creation ideas and to think out financial solutions to step out of poverty (write down your ideas as they come. Have the habit of keeping a pen and a writing pad handy because ideas come in the form of flashes. The smallest pen is bigger and better than the biggest brain); effective inherent individual **talents** as working tools to enhance personal performance for maximum productivity in your chosen career job or occupation from which you earn income. Use your gift of talent to your best ability. Talent that is wasted has no value. Talent that is made into efforts will bring unexpected rewards.

"Everything you need is already in your life awaiting your recognitions of it"- Mike Murdock. In order words, all the initial capital resources that are required for you to start creating financial wealth, and consequently become

financially successful in life is time, brain and talents. Although it all depends on how serious you respond to each of these initial capital resources. One may either prodigally choose to ignore or neglect them or not. However, if you wasteful choose to ignore them you cannot by any means escape the risk of ending up a financial failure. Therefore, to be financially successful or poor in life is a matter of choice for you to either manage or not, these God given initial capital resources. Ask any man who is wealthy and rich, he will tell you that he had never been prodigal in ignoring or wasting his own initial capital resources.

The Biblical prodigal son, having an understanding of this fact made a request from his father to give him the portion of goods that falls to him. In this context the portion of goods that falls to him could mean his own initial capital resources – Brain, Time, and Talents. Then He said: *"A certain man had two sons. And the younger of them said to his father, give me the portion of goods that falls to me; so he divided to them his livelihood"* *(Luk.15v11-12)*. In actual sense, the prodigal son wanted to be independent in making use of his brain, time and talent, not under his father anymore. Eventually, he left with them but wasted them without effectively investing or managing them to do any career job for a source of income, not until it was too late for him.

God also in His fatherhood capacity has these same initial capital resources in abundance from which He had given you your own certain portion of a Time of 24 hours 7 per a week for a year so long as you live; an electrifying creative and resourceful Brain; an effective great inherent gift of Talent; which are all needful for your productive performance in doing any career job. You can only blame yourself if you dare make waste of them and end up a financial failure. Of course, you don't have to be, for it is not meant for you at all. With these available initial capital resources you can move yourself out from the camp of financial poverty in life and join the great league of those who are today in the world creating financial wealth and enjoying riches.

Of course, our great God is never a gold digger who would want to reap where He had not sown. He would never be expecting you to create financial wealth and become rich if He had not made available to you these basic initial capital resources that you require to do so. However, as a child of God, until you lay hold of your own certain portion of the initial capital resources and make effective management of them, you may not be able to create financial wealth. Don't be like the Biblical prodigal son who never made effective management of his but wasted them for nothing in a faraway country. Hence, he failed to create financial wealth but had to live in piggery poverty. Let's consider how you can actually make effective management of your own initial capital resources, so as to be able to utilize them to create financial wealth.

Time: Understand that God in the same equal measure has continued to provide you with a valuable time of 24 hours per day, 7 days per week, and a 4 weeks per each of the 12 months in every year so long as you live. If you must create financial wealth, then you must first learn to understand time and how to manage it well. Understand that you have the same equal time with every other man who has ever lived or are still living. Every man you know who had created or is creating financial wealth today is said to have at his disposal the same time that you too have. You have the same length of equal valuable time in every day of your life just as everyone else anywhere has. Engage your valuable time usefully. Make use of your valuable time to fully engage yourself particularly in doing your career job and improving on your performance in doing it. Also, you may as well usefully spend your time in anything else that has an exchangeable value.

Engage yourself in using your available time to do things that has value which is either useful to you or to others. Use your time to do things that are exchangeable in value for money. As often said that time is money. The usage of your time should have a quantifiable value whether of monetary, spiritual, academic, social etc. Learn to do the right thing at the right time. Don't waste your time on doing the wrong things. On daily, weekly, monthly or yearly basis, assign your schedules and activities wisely to the material time at your disposal. You can learn more from books on time management, it will help you to harness your time in order to make good use of it to create financial wealth. Please look for and get such books that deals with time management.

However, it is equally important that you develop a quick response attitude to time. Because every time wasted is time lost and is never regained back again. Someone once said that every second just as every incident is as significant as every day that passes on in one's life. And another said, you can make more money but you can't make more time. Time is the greatest assets with the highest rate of depreciation. It is the greatest gift to offer to someone who is still alive. Time is a free resource equally given to all men without partiality. It is one of the available initial capital resources from God. Time as a free capital resource provides man the greatest opportunities to become a great achiever of financial success in life. But if you become prodigal of time, then the greatest opportunities to create your desired financial wealth may become wasted. The usage of your time reveals your most priorities in life. If creating financial wealth is a priority to you, then you better direct your time towards it.

The greatest enemy that targets to waste a man's time in order to either stop or delay him from his pursuit to achieve any meaningful financial success is **Procrastination.** Hear what *Benjamin Franklin* has to say about procrastination, *"Never put off till tomorrow that which you can do today"*. *George Washington* puts it this way, *"ninety-nine percent of failures come from people who have the habit of making excuses"*. An excuse is the anchor that holds the ship of financial success at bay of delay. Procrastination is nothing but a mere excuse or couple of excuses that sometimes arises out of: ignorant attitude of wanting to wait for a state of perfection, misplacement of priority and fear *(Luk.14v17-20)*. *"The men with excuses discover every conceivable reason why a course will fail"- David Schwartz.*

The Psalmist having understood the dangers of procrastination did earnestly beseeched God to teach him how he would number his days with wisdom. This he needed so that he would know what to do in each day of his life in order to achieve all the dimensions of prosperity inclusive of financial wealth while here on earth before his departure to eternity. In fact, you should not be prodigal (wasteful) of your time by chosen to be resting your future in procrastination, because time itself does not rest. According to *Tolstoy*, *"Time is infinite movement without one movement of rest"*.

You must agree that NOW, no other time behind it or

ahead of it is the most appropriate time for you to rise up on your feet to pursue to create financial wealth as a dimension of prosperity that you deserve. If you don't accept the fact that now is the time, then when else? Folding your arms to wait for something, say this or that to happen before you can step out of the territory of financial failure is totally an act of delaying your time. It is not befitting to you at all. For you can't just afford to over stay before becoming a man or a woman of great financial achievements.

Brain: Your situation of not yet being able to create financial wealth may never change until you begin to make use of your brain both to think out financial solution and to generate financial wealth creation seed of ideas. Your ideas are your greatest assets in life. Perhaps you are right now anchoring at the bay of poverty. You really need to take off sailing from there by making use of your electrifying creative brain to think positively and to generate ideas on ways out of poverty. Your brain is one of your creative free gifted resources that have the rich potential and capacity to help you to create financial wealth. Many today are financially poor, not because they could not create financial wealth but because they failed to creatively make good use of their God given brain.

The capacity and potential of our brain has always been under applied and consequently under-utilized by many.

Man has always been guilty of making a full waste of his brain which leads to financial poverty. Through your subconscious, your creative thinking activates the brain cells to generate possible wealth creation ideas that are great and valuable enough not only for you to solve your problem of financial poverty but also to create financial wealth. Your brain is your greatest creative resource at your disposal for you to create financial wealth. *According to Ayn Rand, "wealth is the product of man's capacity to think".* And someone else says, *"There is no shortage of money on this planet, only a shortage of people who think correctly about it".* Of course, the thinking is done with the brain. Truly, God has not given you the brain only for you to lock it up. No, He gave it to you to help you think out great ideas through it.

Therefore, learn how to make use of your brain to make financial thinking, create financial solution, and generate valuable investment and financial ideas by which you would be able to create financial wealth. Don't leave it idle – use your brain as a capital resource for creating financial wealth. Remember, no one pays for having brain; but life rewards those who use theirs intelligently. In life, it is not what you don't have that limits you; it is what you have but don't know how to use. Your brain is the storehouse of the most valuable wealth-creation ideas for financial success. Your financial success is stocked up in your brain. Utilize your own brain like others did and make good use of it to create financial wealth. When your brain is creatively engaged to work, your mind too becomes mentally developed to generate up the required ideas. Both becomes ready to actively work together to enable you achieve financial success. Therefore, harness, utilize and make good use of your creative brain and mental mind to make financial riches a reality experience in your life.

Effectiveness brings results while efficiency saves costs. Whatever is not for usage will most likely be for waste. Your brain, time and talents are given to you for effective management and efficient usage not for careless waste. To waste a thing is to make prodigal of it. And to be prodigal simply means to live a wasteful life. Unless you effectively and efficiently engage and invest your brain, time and talents to do a career job from which you earn income, you may be unable to take advantage of financial opportunities that may come your way.

Whatever you don't know its value you would easily seem to despise and make waste of that same thing. Your brain, time and talent are all of great value that you should not despise or waste them. Note that, God is not wasteful in nature. Imagine, the oxygen to carbon-dioxide exchange between man and plants is a master piece of God's act of thrift and shrewdness. God further demonstrated this fact through Christ when He fed the five thousand multitudes. He instructed His disciples to gather up all the remains and left-overs *(Math. 14v20)*. He never wanted any portion of the left-overs and fallen crumbs to be wasted at all.

Unlike the Biblical prodigal son, who by his act of wasteful living violated this principle which Christ too did apply. The Scripture accounted for this thus, *"And not many days after the younger son gathered all together, journeyed to a far country, and there wasted his possessions (time, brain and talents) with Prodigal living" (Luke15 v 13)*. The prodigal son foolishly made a total waste of the certain portion of his own supposed brain, time and talent without usefully engaging them to do any career job from which he would have been able to earn money. Out of his despising attitude and neglect, he extravagantly lavished and wasted his brain in dormancy, talents in idleness, time in frivolity or trivial activities without actively engaging them to do any career job that could have fetched him money to create financial wealth.

No doubt, his prodigal living might have been caused by peers influence in the far country. You too must be mindful of who your friends are if you really want to create financial wealth. His love of the world and things in the world might have been another factor of influence *(I John 2 v 15-17)*. I could sense he was busy indulging himself in all sorts of ill and risky lifestyle perhaps such as smoking, alcoholism, clubbing, fornication, gambling, etc. These forms of indulgencies can take you on to the pathway of wasting your brain, time and talents to do nothing that could earn you money. He costly toyed with the portion of his own brain, time and talent. And he dearly suffered for it.

Definitely, any man that makes waste of them is bound to achieve financial failure in life. You can't be wasting your God given wonderful brain, wasting your talents, wasting your time to do nothing and still want to create financial wealth *(Prb.21v20)*. It won't be possible at all. No man has ever thrown an axe head into a river and still gets it back. It would only take Elisha's miracle for that to happen. That is the miracle of magnetic "U" turn from the river of the life of prodigality. Unless this happens, any man who is making waste of his own brain, time and talent to do no career job will sooner or later face the unfortunate and terrible condition of financial famine in life. And just before he may know it, he will already have gotten headlong deep into sticking poverty and mediocrity.

Principle of avoidance of financial famine

If you fail to avoid causing something that is dangerous and destructive, you may end up becoming a victim of that very thing. You must avoid causing financial famine for yourself. Else you may become a victim of its painful experience. *"But when he had spent all, there arose a severe famine in that land and he began to be in want" (Luke 15 v 14)*. The big question here I suppose is, what must have happened to the prodigal son that he found himself being in financial lack? The answer to the above question is obvious. He caused financial famine for himself. *Financial famine is a miserable and pitiable state of financial failure where you continue to wastefully live your life without usefully engaging your brain, time and talents to do nothing either as a career job or handiwork which consequently either leads to a period or to a life time of poverty experience.* A period of poverty experience could be a terrible one for anyone.

A period of poverty experience is a period when you live your life in total lack of financial ability: to afford your basic needs or necessities of life let alone affording any comfort facilities; to take care of your extended responsibilities; to acquire and possess financial or material assets and let alone to making a business investment. It is truly a terrible experience for one to pass through. Whenever you choose to live your life doing nothing, you are just about causing yourself a financial famine that will eventually lead you into a period of poverty experience. Unfortunately, even many Christians are wallowing in this terrible period. Why, perhaps because they have allowed themselves to be caught up in the web of prodigality where they have continued to live to waste either their hard earned money or their brain, time and talents to do nothing as a handiwork or career job.

If you cause yourself financial famine, it won't be long you will become a heavy financial parasite that is solely dependent on others for financial survival in life. This, later became the case of the prodigal son who caused himself financial famine. He consequently stepped into a period of poverty experience because he wasted his cash at hand together with his brain, time and talent doing nothing for the first couple of years that he went to a far country. Hence, he began to labor and struggle to work so hard for others for his financial survival. He became a parasitic dependent on leftovers of pigs' feed for his survival and living. *"And he would gladly have filled his stomach with the pods that the swine ate, and no one gave him anything" (Luk.15v16).* It will always end in this same ugly way for you too if you cause financial famine for yourself. I pray it won't be your portion.

CHAPTER THIRTEEN

PRINCIPLES FOR CREATING FINANCIAL WEALTH 11

Principle of savings

And what is it that you have to save if you really want to create financial wealth in life. Obviously it is money. And where would this money come from? As a matter of fact, you must set a personal financial policy of making a periodic savings out of the income you are earning from your career job. A man who would not save a penny of money is a man who will sink into poverty soon. If you want to create financial wealth and become rich, then you must always endeavor to save some part of your income. However, it is imperative to point out here that sometimes you can get what I call un-worked income such as grants of money, gifts of money or such free monies from others. These are income that comes either on the basis of friendship and relationship, assistance and support or obligation to you from others that you have not contractually worked for.

As a matter of financial principle for creating financial wealth, you are expected to save some part of your income regardless of how much little your income may be. You must not be spending all your income on consumptions alone. A penny savings from your income (including any un-worked income) can actually go a long way to help you to gradually begin to create financial wealth. Your today's savings shapes your tomorrow's income and that determines your future financial success. How extent you would create financial wealth depends on how much savings you can make out of your income for investment.

In order to escape this ugly situation, you must seek for and engage yourself into a source of income career job. From the career job no matter how a little penny your income may be, always make at least a digit savings out of it today to enable you take advantages of tomorrow's investment opportunities for you to experience financial miracle. Perhaps with just one or few financial opportunity (ies) across your life, you can be sure of creating financial wealth in the most nearest future. Your saved income put you in a financial position required to take advantage of investment opportunity in order to experience a financial miracle. Yet what you need first to do is to make savings out of your income if you must get prepared for a financial miracle.

However, investment opportunity is one of the ways through which God returns financial reward to a man. This, God does especially to those who sincerely are partnering with Him to be a financial blessing to others in need and to the church for the financing of His kingdom work. God is so much interested in bringing across your way an investment opportunity for you to take advantage of it. Yet it depends on how much you are prepared to take advantage of it so as to make a financial miracle happen in your life.

Nevertheless, *financial miracle is a state of an unexpected inflow of returnable incomes or release of financial buoyancy arising from an investment whether of small or big nature by which you become either financially independent, abundant or able to meet your financial needs, responsibilities and or obligations either for a period of time or for a life time.* Financial miracle can last for a life time but only when it is managed well. You can qualify to experience and witness financial miracle only when you have prepared for it. However, note that any inflow of income or release of financial buoyance arising from crime, stealing or robbery, fraud or dupe, bribery and embezzlement is never a financial miracle; but a *"financial muzzling"* of other people's money. So, if your income is coming by way of financial muzzling, don't forget that it is accursed and attracts God's judgment.

Meanwhile, financial miracle happens only in the life of those who are prepared for it. God won't open heavens to release bundle of thousands of dollars for you to experience financial miracle. What God owes you is to bring across to you certain investment opportunities on the ground that you should be wise enough to have set aside a portion of saved income with which to take advantage of it. Meanwhile, when you are not yet prepared to take advantage of an investment opportunity, it may come to you several times but you may still not be able to take advantage of it for you to experience financial miracle. Of course, you don't have to wait for God to ask you to save part of your income. He expects you to be wiser than serpent just as He is too.

Hence, financial miracle is a factor of your ability to use your saved income or your portion of money set aside to position yourself financially to be able to take advantage of any available but viable investment opportunity. Always deploy your reasoning and analytical ability besides your acquired financial and economic info-knowledge to be able to identify wisely such existing investment opportunities as well as to ascertain their viability. You must be sensitive, analytical and informed enough to discover and identify an investment opportunity that is available around you.

An investment opportunity if you take advantage of it is bound to give you high returnable income either in a short or long period of time. While another existing investment opportunity may only give you low returnable income if you take advantage of it. Some of the investment opportunities may require either huge or small capital for you to take advantage of them. No matter the level of your savings as capital, you would always see around you an existing investment opportunity that your savings or money at your disposal can match with.

Hear what *Louis Pasteur* says that *chance favors the prepared mind*. The chance here refers to investment opportunity which will favor you only when you are prepared (have a set aside portion of money or savings from your income) to take advantage of it. Another wise saying has it that miracle happens when preparation meets with opportunity. *The wise man Solomon crowned it up by saying, "I returned and saw under the sun that — the race is not for the swift, nor the battle for the strong, nor bread for the wise, nor riches to men of understanding, nor favor to men of skill; but time (preparation) and chance (opportunity) happen to them all".*

Most people today who are richer than you never became financially rich without getting themselves prepared with certain portion of a set aside income whether as inherited or as savings made over a period of time. They actually used it to take advantage of certain investment opportunities, and today they have eventually succeeded in creating financial wealth. That might be the difference between you and them. Financial miracle can happen in your life if you too can get yourself prepared and position yourself to take advantage of any of the ever emerging investment opportunities. God can bring one or two of it across to you. And that will change your story forever and your life for better. Of course, you need an open door of financial position (periodic savings from your money income) to enable you experience a financial miracle that can put you on the fastest lane of creating financial wealth, such that can give you the highest level of financial ability. And the above fact is the more reason why you need a career job from which you can be earning periodic money income.

However, an opportunity is a rare open chance that is available for someone to take advantage of it within a given time frame. Opportunities are never endless but are always rare. Opportunities are for everybody but never wait for anybody. Opportunities are always available for those who are already prepared and ready to take advantage of them. In every day, week, month and year, God do create and make investment opportunities available for us to utilize and take advantage of them in order to enable us to create financial wealth. No one has ever lived on earth that had not come across certain investment opportunities in life.

Your ability to respond to such investment opportunities as they appear and taking advantage of them will definitely contribute and determine a lot and to a large extent on how far you will be able to create financial wealth. The wise man Solomon discovered this truth as he saw it under the sun that creating financial wealth is not to men of understanding but it is time and chance (opportunity) that could make it become a reality in a man's life *(Ecc.9v11)*. Note here that opportunities are product of time. They come just as time goes by. In other words, at every time there are certain investment opportunities availably awaiting with a limited time for someone to take advantage of.

As important as God would create and make certain investment opportunities available for you, so also it is for you to recognize or discover them as they come by. Otherwise another may discover or take notice of the same investment opportunities and take advantage of them before you. God is ever so magnanimous to create and make these investment opportunities available for you to be able to create financial wealth. For He alone is the God of times and seasons who actively rules in the whole affairs of men. He allows certain things to happen without which certain other things that bring opportunities may not happen. For this reason, God makes all things to work together for your good. So it is left for you to search for such rare open and available investment opportunities, identify and discover them on time, and take advantage of them but never waste them. They are everywhere at all time around you but never wait for you endlessly.

Principle of risk-taking to invest

"Your future is created by what you do today, not tomorrow. The

main cause of poverty is fear and ignorance, the cause is not the government, the economy or rich people. Self-inflicted fear and ignorance keeps people broke. I have never met a rich person who has never lost money but I have met a lot of poor people who has never lost a dime. The primary difference between the rich and the poor is how they handle fear in investment" - *Robert Kiyosaki.* Someone said that FEAR means, *"Forget Everything And Rise or Face Everything And Rise". "Once you become fearless, life becomes limitless – Tai Lopez.*

If there is any risk worth taking in life, it is the financial risk to make investment. Yes, it always appears financially risk to invest money. Especially when such money is one's savings over a period of time. *Risk is the doorway of success – Don Ortiz. "The greatest mistake a man can make is to be afraid of making one. You never fail until you stop trying"- Elbert Hubbard.* Risk is the probability of possible results or outcomes which may either be bad and unpleasant such as loss and failure; or good and pleasant such as gain and success. *"People who focus on their fear don't grow. They become paralyzed"- John C. Maxwell.* Someone says, *"If you fail, never give up because the word 'FAIL' simply means 'First Attempt In Learning'. End is not the end, in fact END means 'Effort Never Dies". If you get no as an answer, remember, 'NO' means 'Next Opportunity'. So be positive to take risk". "Be bold when you see opportunity. If you are afraid, you will never get rich – Robert Kuok, Malaysian richest man.*

A man still wanting to avert taking financial risk to invest is a man not yet determined to create financial wealth. Even the Eagle do take great risk to ensure that its eaglets learn how to fly successfully in the air: The eagle removes the feathers and soft grass in her nest in order to expose her younger ones to discomfort and force them to go into a risky adventure of flying; of which they eventually do fly when it becomes totally unbearable for them to stay in the nest. Until you become uncomfortable with your state of poverty, you may not be ready to take risk to come out of poverty. *"He who is not courageous enough to take risks will accomplish nothing in life" – Muhammaad Ali.* The future belongs to the risk takers, not the comfort seekers.

"Men who never take chances in life, never get ahead in life"- Robert Schuller. Risk is part of life, virtually everything we do involves risk and one must be ready to take it. The blessed late Arch. *Bishop Idahosa says, "It is very risk not to take risk".* It is better to take risk in life than to avert it. Because in taking risk, riches are made for wealth to be created. *"The cave you fear to enter holds the treasure that you seek" – Joseph Campbell.* If you don't take risk you will never learn how to manage risk. *"To win big, you sometimes have to take big risks" – Bill Gates.* With a positive oriented mind you must be prepared to take financial risk to invest your money without being deterred by its possible outcome, whether it will end up turning out a failure or a success, a loss or a

gain. *"Don't let the fear of losing be greater than the excitement of winning" – Robert kiyosaki.* Even if you take financial risk and fail, then hear this, *"Failure is normal and most champions have known it before success"- Chris E. K.*

Bill W. Wayman says, "To fail is not shameful but to be a failure is more shameful. It is better to fail at something than to succeed at nothing". The greatest risk of avoiding taking financial risk to invest your saved income is the highest risk of missing out some great investment opportunities to create financial wealth. *"You don't concentrate on risk, you concentrate on results"- Chuck Yeager.* There is much to learn in taking risk than to averting it. When you take risk you learn your mistakes and gather more experiences on how you will make a better and perfect launch or outing again than you had done or could do before. *"Failure is the only opportunity to move intelligently and begin again"- Henry Ford.* Your destiny goal to create financial wealth should be able to breed inside of you the readiness to take financial risk to make investment that can get you out of poverty.

Dare to take risks in your life. If you gain, you can lead others to it; if you loss, you can guide others out of it. There is no joy in victory without running the risk of defeat. If you really want to create financial wealth, then you must step out to take financial risk to invest your money in order to diversify your income.

You must set yourself on motion to get to the financial wealth creation destination, where you are required to make strategic and conservative investments for a yield of returnable income that could last for life. Of course, the only way to avert the risk of ending up living your life in the dungeon of poverty and mediocrity is to take financial risk to make right investment of your money. Meanwhile, those who have created financial wealth and are today living to enjoy riches had always taken financial risk to invest substantial amount of money either saved or borrowed. Ask them, and they will tell you.

Of course, for now that you are about to start, you may not even need to take the financial risk to borrow huge amount of a million dollar for you to invest. What you may need now is to take the financial risk to borrow maybe just some amount of dollar either in hundred or thousand units. I am sure that most of the world renowned men of riches never created their empire of financial wealth without taking the financial risk to borrow money to invest more and more. At their starting stage I doubt whether their amount of borrowed money were in millions of dollars. Sure, they must have borrowed either only in hundred or in thousand units of amount of dollar.

The important thing may not be how huge you want to

borrow money to invest. I guess the most important thing is for you to make up your mind to take financial risk to borrow at least even a little money to invest. However, note that borrowing money to invest is never the best option, for it is costly because it attracts a payable interest and goes with a high risk. Especially as an investment beginner. Borrowing money to invest should only be considered an option where your own savings or disposable income won't be enough for your choice or size of investment. It may also be an option when you are certainly sure that the investment you seek to make will scale through to yield expected returns. Thirdly, borrowing may still be an option when it has become unavoidably necessary for you to expand an already existing viable business investment, basically for the purpose of creating more market or meeting up with emerging demand, in order to increase income returns. More so, your option to borrow may actually depend on the kind or the hugeness of the investment you want to make.

Take note, to borrow too huge an amount of money may land you into financial liquidation. Therefore, always be analytically guided and well informed on which of the existing investment opportunities is the most viable and has the best earning worth for you to make an investment especially with borrowed money.

Thus the word of God says, *"Do not remember the former*

things nor consider the things of old. Behold I will do a new thing ..." (Is.43v18-19). God is always interested and ever ready to do a new thing in our lives even in our income. You too can do a new thing concerning your current income status. You can create a new stream of income and you would remember no more your current income status. Hence, your current income status will become a thing of old. Don't ever be comfortable with your current income status but don't as well be crazy and unmoral to create a new stream of income status that is from a wrong source. You need a new stream of income status to be able to seize further investment opportunities for income diversification, which is required for an expanded new income flow.

Principle of investment for income diversification

From financial wealth creation perspective, it does not alone end up at you earning money or making savings but more important than that is what you do with it. Many do earn money and make savings but not many do invest them. Some do earn money and make savings and still do spend them up on trivial things. You are under obligation as a matter of financial principle to make right and appropriate investment of your portion of earning or savings. In order to create financial wealth, you must be committed to investing part of your current money income to create a new stream of money income in return.

The economics equation says that money income is equal to consumption plus savings. And savings is equal to investment. While the equation for your current money income is expressed as thus above, the equation for your new streams of money income can be expressed as the current consumption plus current savings equal to current investment plus new returnable incomes from old investment. Without current earnings and savings you won't make investment and without investment you won't be able to build up and create a new stream of returnable income besides your current income.

When you want to be rich for just a year, then only save money through your fixed paid-income and then after a while you become a spending consumer who will end up a poor man. But when you want to be rich for life, then build a bank of financial wealth for yourself through investment, then after a while you become money earner who will end up a rich man. And why do you need to invest today to diversify your income source or inflow? It's because the older you get, the more expensive and money-demanding life becomes. You would need money to pay bills; to acquire mortgages; to purchase car; to pay for education; to spend for medications; to settle debts; to afford comfort; to offer financial assistance or help to relatives or friends; and to make donations for humanitarian, charity or community work.

When the eagle grows old, its feathers becomes weak and can neither take it faster nor as higher as it should. This makes the eagle weak and could make it die too. So it would retire to a solitary place far away on the mountain. While there, the eagle plucks out its weak feathers from its body and breaks its beaks and claws against the rocks until it is completely bare; a very bloody and painful process. Then it stays in this hiding place until it has grown new feathers, new beaks and claws and then it comes out flying higher than before. Accept the fact that you are growing old by the day. You can't be at the same financial position year-in year-out.

Go for a new bigger business or job; and new line of investment for you to diversify and increase your income streams. Your fixed salary alone cannot be enough to take care of all your financial needs and responsibilities especially as you grow older in life. *Robert Mugabe*, the immediate past President of Zimbabwe once said, *"When your salary comes in time, you eat chicken. As the salary reduces you eat products of chicken – eggs and subsequently you begin to eat chicken's food – maize and millet, and finally, when salary is finished, you become chicken itself, spending your time walking around just looking for what to eat".*

The simple relative message to the above statement is that, at your stage of singleness before the age of 25 or 30 to your marriage consummation, with salary alone you would live in financial plenty; at the era of arrival of children, with salary alone you would live in financial moderation; at the age of multiple expenditure for accruing bills, family upkeep, children education, unforeseen emergencies, with salary alone you would live in financial struggling; and at the retiring age in life, with salary alone you would live in financial dependence as a liability to others. But with other streams of income flow besides your salary the story would be totally different.

Endeavour to seek to expand your streams of income: to be able to meet your daily needs; to be able to afford your needed comfort facilities; to be able to acquire material and financial assets; and to be able to multiply your investment horizon to become a man of great financial wealth. Take this time to shake off the financial yoke and shackles upon your life. Also, prune and pluck out the things that bound you to poverty. No one will pluck the feathers of poverty out from you, except you. You may need to isolate yourself from all your past financial errors, mistakes, and bondage for you to be able to completely shade off your old poverty feathers, which have not allowed you to fly at the highest altitude of financial wealth.

Never depend on single income. Never test the depth of a river with both feet. That could be too risky. Do not put all your eggs in one basket. Make investment to create a stream source of income. Income diversification leads to income multiplication. If you want to create financial wealth, then you need not to stop only at creating just a one new income stream. You still need to move on further to explore other options of new investment opportunities available wherein you can reinvest your whole new stream of income or part of it so as to diversify your income generation and inflow. Never should you channel your new stream of income to consumption alone.

"Honestly, if I have the resources to become wealthier, I will rather invest it, than save it up. Savings doesn't increase your net worth, it stagnates your opportunity to have more. The best way to save is to invest multiple streams of income platform, because the money is out of your reach, and it's bringing in more and you wouldn't be tempted to spend it" – Donald Trump. Invest a portion of your income. And be patient to see it grow. If what you have in your hands is not good to be called a harvest then it's a seed, sow it into investment.

You can invest your money either to establish a brand new entrepreneurial business, business investment and or to acquire an already consolidated one or become a co-owner or shareholder of such a one. You can begin your investment with small petty buying and selling business outlet. You may as well invest your earning or savings in seasonal storage business whereby you buy certain seasonal goods at low prices and resell them when their prices go higher. Also there are existing good opportunities for you to invest in financial assets business such as buying of stocks, debentures, treasury bills, and or other fixed time interest-yielding deposit. Great investment opportunities is equally existing in the area of network marketing business. You can as well invest in the transport and distribution business. There are emerging opportunities for investment in the ICT sector. Better still if you have the financial capacity to venture into full time manufacturing, production and or processing industry business.

The money that you needed to invest may come from your earning or savings over a period of time or borrowed money from friends, parents, thrift group or social club to which you belong, bank or from other financial institutions. Such borrowed money can always be lent to you either as a zero interest loan or as an interest payable loan or overdraft in case of bank. However, to borrow money to invest involves a high risk. In fact, to borrow money for investment is risky in the sense that you may not be able to repay the borrowed money if the investment eventually fails and you incur loss. You can only be able to repay it if the investment eventually succeeds and you make gains.

However, know that wealth and riches is never lottery that you can win neither is it a jackpot that you can hit at by luck. No! Not all. Financial wealth is a dimension of prosperity that you must work hard to create in life. You don't just wish for it, and just get to it. You must dearly want to own and possess financial wealth, and then work hard to create it. Of course, investment is the key to creating financial wealth. Investment is like an economic assets purchased today for the purpose of creating a steady income flow tomorrow.

With an investment idea your salary or your fixed-time income becomes financial instrument by which you can create financial freedom through a long time business investment that could guarantee a life time steady inflows of residual income, not only for you but also for your children. It is the financial freedom you create for yourself at your youthful age that allows you to continue to earn income even when you had retired from active engagement either in paid work or self-owned business.

Every state of the economy offers investment opportunities for men with an investment idea to create financial wealth. In fact, recession is often a time to create financial wealth by those who could grab the opportunities that it offers. There has never been a recession period that everybody is poor. And there has never been a prosperous year that everybody is rich. Poverty and riches are products of choice.

Therefore, learn to spot around you investment opportunities to create financial wealth. And when you spot one, take action at once to give birth to an investment idea that would enable you to take advantage of it. When action meets an investment opportunity, it results to financial miracle. But hear this, *"Opportunities are like sunrises. If you wait too long, you miss it"* – *William Arthur Ward.* So, be ever ready to take action when you see opportunities for you to create financial wealth. *"Successful leaders have to take the courage to take action while others hesitates"* – *John Maxwell.* Someone says, *"The distance between dreams and reality is called action. Do it now. Sometimes 'Later' becomes 'Never'". "Knowledge will enrich you, but only action will turn it into riches"* – *Darren Hardy.* Do it now

And when an investment opportunity meets with an investment idea, it absolutely becomes possible to create financial wealth. *Steve Jobs* came up with one investment idea for financial wealth creation; and that's IPhone. *Bill Gates* also came up with one investment idea for financial wealth creation; and that's Windows Operating System. Imagine! Just one investment idea from God can actually become an investment opportunity for you to create stinky financial wealth. The man who would enjoy financial success is one who can without delay grab the bricks of investment opportunities that others have thrown away. Life will never provide warranties and guarantees. It can only provide possibilities and opportunities. It's up to you to take advantage of them and convert them into financial wealth.

The world has much of investment opportunities to offer; carefully and consciously explore them. And you will discover that there are some of them you could take advantage of with your investment idea. And every time you try something new, you will not only learn more about yourself but also add more value to yourself. The journey into the new world of creating financial wealth, and new possibilities of becoming rich is mostly by remaining sensitive to investment opportunities and open-minded to investment ideas. Try to come up with a new investment idea every day and you will migrate far away from poverty. An investment idea simply means, knowing what you can personally create or do which has an economic or exchangeable value that could become an investment or business operation from which you earn money to create financial wealth. An investment opportunity is knowing when there is an existing rare timed-chance that is economically and financially viable for you to invest your earning or savings. While an investment information is knowing when there are and what are the existing investment opportunities and which exactly to invest your earning or savings that has a higher prospect of earning worth.

Be absolutely positive about investment. You never can create financial wealth if you are too scared of losing money. Of course salary alone cannot solve your money problems. You need a secondary source of income to balance up. Someone says, "Salary is medicine for managing poverty, it doesn't cure it. Only your business or investment cures poverty". Hears this, *"You can't use prayer to replace laziness. No investment means no return"* – T. D. Jakes.

You owe yourself the responsibility to always think wisely and evaluate other options of investment opportunities available and consider using either or both of your money income, savings, and new income stream with an investment idea to take advantage of them. You must avoid negotiating for the risk of putting all your eggs in one basket. They can all break at once. Diversify your investment today to expand your source of income tomorrow. By so doing, you will be able to escape in your life the risk of not surviving any unexpected fatal income-source accident.

Principle of networking business

Today the networking industry business is a fast growing one. Though the industry is being threatened with and pirated by a lot of networking scam and Ponzi business schemes. Therefore, be sure to go into a networking business that proves to be real, reliably secure, and viably sustainable with a rewarding financial prospect that suits your drive to create financial wealth. Going into networking industry business requires that you have adequate knowledge of it, how it works and how best you can take advantage of it to make financial fortune. Also, you must have the required online marketing or salesman skill to either market the product you are dealing on; expand the number of your referrals; or grow your network tree to a highest possible level. One thing with networking industry business is that it doesn't just grow overnight. Patience is required of anyone who must be successful in networking business.

Thus, *Robert Kiyosaki* says it all better, *"If someone invites you to join a network marketing business, join the business even if you don't know what it is all about. But be patient and learn the process gradually and relentlessly. Remain there even if it takes you five years to be successful in it because when the benefits begin to flow, you will never be the same person ever again".* Unfortunately, people don't always have the patience to build especially a networking business for 3 years. But they do have the patience to go to work for 40 years.

Globally this industry business has continued to offer thousands of investment opportunities to a great number of men and women. Unfortunately, many are lacking the investment idea to take the advantage of the investment opportunities that this emerging industry business offers. Yet many others who have seized these investment opportunities are millionaires today. Consider the following comments made by some successful rich men who have either benefited from the networking industry business or aware of the huge potential opportunities that is offering for financial wealth creation.

"Network Marketing is the fastest growing business of 21st century which must be joined by every young man and woman globally otherwise you can never get the best of your youth age" – *Dr. A. P. J. Abdul Kalam.*

"Network Marketing is the future business in India. This is the 21st century and this business will give the revenue of 9,000 core to Indian government till 2025" – *Ram Vilas Paswan.*

"The Network Marketing industry in India estimated to be INR billion (2012-13), and forms only around 0.4% of total retail sales. This industry has the potential to reach size of INR 645 billion by 2025" – *FICCI & KPMG.*

"If I would be given a chance to start all over again, I would choose network marketing" – *Bill Gates.*

Network Marketing has produced more millionaires than any other industry in the history of world" – *Les Brown.*

"You strengthen our country and our economy not just by striving for your own success but by offering the opportunity (network marketing) to others" – *Bill Clinton.*

"Network Marketing gives people the opportunity with very low risk and very low financial commitment to build their own income generating asset and acquire great wealth" – *Robert Kiyosaki.*

"When you talk about network marketing being a better way, you will face rejection by ignorant people" – *Eric Worre.*

"In network marketing you will think the reward is money, but the freedom will far outweigh the money and in the end it will be all about the lives you change" – *Paula Pritchard.*

CHAPTER FOURTEEN

DARE TO BECOME A HIRER OF LABOUR

Hire others than to be hired by others

After a long time that the prodigal son had lived his life wasting his time, brain and talent doing nothing to earn any money but lavishly spent and caused financial famine for himself. Eventually he stepped into a period of poverty experience in which he had no option than to labor and struggle to work for a citizen of that country.

The worst he could do for himself was to take up the menial job of feeding the swine. That is a situation of laboring for others. What a financial failure that instead of creating financial wealth to be able to afford himself with at least a good taste of food and comfort facilities in life. He could only feed on the smelling left-over pods that swine had fed on. *"Then he went and joined himself to a citizen of that country, and he sent him into his fields to feed swine" (Luke15v 15).* Despite the daily maximum input of his brain, time and talent – skills and knowledge to struggle and labor hard for a citizen of that country who had a piggery farm, he was only able to have a minimal financial survival and sustenance.

"But when, he came back to himself, he said, How many of my father's hired servants have bread enough and to spare, and I perish

with hunger! I will arise and go to my father, and will say to him," father..., Make me like one of your hired servants" (Luke 15 v 17-19).

The devastating poverty experience that the prodigal son had, did leave him in Frustration, Shame, Mediocrity, Confusion, Lost of social Relevance, Misery, Mockery, Abuse, Disappointment, Victimization, Denial of Right, Stagnation, Un-fulfillment, etc. This sort of experience can leave you with no or little happiness, peace, hope, comfort and relaxation in life. It was this experience that made him to actually come back to his senses. He decided to arise and get back to his father with a new road-map-proposal. The proposal was, "make me like one of your hired servants". He was ready to offer himself to be employed by his father as one of his hired servants. Truly he had become used to being a hired servant who would labor to work hard for others.

Meanwhile, his father having a better knowledge of what it takes for one to create lasting financial wealth did have his own different proposal for him. His father's proposal was, "it is better for you to judiciously make hiring of your brain, time and talent – skills and knowledge to become an employer of yourself. That's having your own self-created job no matter how small it may be than for you to be a hired servant (laborer or worker) who will labor only to work hard for others". Being a hired employee or worker is a situation in life where you are engaged as a servant by a master (a hirer of labor) to make an input of your brain, energy, time, talent - developed skills and knowledgeable ability to labor and work for him in order to earn a pay of income that may only or may not guarantee a financial survival without a 100% guarantee for a long term financial self-sustenance.

In most cases, the only option for you especially in a period of poverty experience is to labor and struggle to work hard for others only for you to earn a pay of income for your financial survival alone. However, the financial mindset and orientation of the prodigal son's father is that a hired servant can labor and work hard to do his career job to earn a pay of income for financial survival which alone won't be enough for sustenance. But he that hires others who labor to work for him will earn substantial flow of income return on his investment. Such income return on investment can actually afford he who had hired others the financial ability to take care of his basic daily needs, sustain his family in comfort, and to take advantage of every available investment opportunities.

Those who hire others to earn profit as income do have better chances to create financial wealth faster than those who are hired to be servants or workers. For they are only entitled to receive a fixed income pay. Meaning that, there are two categories of people who are entitled to financial earnings. First is the employee (worker or laborer) who as a servant is hired with other partnering colleagues to labor and to work hard for a periodic financial reward of an income pay from an employer (owners or investors). Second is the employer who as a master had in the time past independently invested his savings or earnings to establish or acquire an operational business investment.

Hired employees are only entitled to earn a periodic income pay. Unlike the employers who are entitled to earn income returns. The hired workers are paid from the riches of financial wealth of the hirer of workers. But the hirer of employees independently controls the riches of his financial wealth. You can now imagine why the father of the prodigal son wouldn't engage his son as one of his hired workers. He rather wanted him to take after him as a hirer of workers so that he can create and control his own financial wealth than to be paid from another's own. It is rather quite unfortunate that even multitude of nations' citizens are still laboring and struggling in their lives to work tirelessly hard for others only to earn an income pay for their financial survival.

An income pay can only be enough not for your financial sustenance but for your financial survival and perhaps for a limited savings. But earning of income returns that comes from an already owned entrepreneurial business or investment can take you beyond financial survival and offer you the financial ability to sustain and to diversify your investment. No one has ever created financial wealth only with a periodic income pay. However, earning income returns may obviously be the best starting point for you towards creating financial wealth in life. Think of all the men of riches you know, they are all hirer of labor who are earners of income returns from their owned conglomerate businesses or investments.

Sometimes it is possible that you can be a hired worker entitled to earn an income pay and at the same time be a hirer of labor also entitled to earn income returns. You can be a hired employee to others from whom you earn certain income pay and equally at the same time be a hirer of other workers who earn from you certain income pay. If at all you want to create financial wealth, no matter the hugeness of your entitled earning of an income pay, you must never all through your life choose to engage your brain, time and talent only to work as a hired employee who would labor and work for a hirer of labor. Your income pay can't just only be enough for you to create the level of financial wealth that can entirely get you rich out of poverty. You must seek to actively engage your brain, time and talent more in your own business in order to change your fixed salary income.

Hear the sayings of *Jack MA*, *"If you put bananas and money in front of Monkeys, monkeys will choose bananas because monkeys do* not know that money can buy a lot of bananas. In reality, if you offer job and business to people, they would choose job because most people do not know that business can bring more money than wages.

In other words, don't limit yourself only to your career job. You can only become a hirer of labor by establishing an entrepreneurial venture and or business investment. *"A job means you're being paid to mind somebody else's business. In this new economy, you need to mind your own business"* – Robert Kiyosaki. This is the only way to take yourself out of sole dependence on salary alone. It is better for you to work harder to hire others to work for you; than for you to work hard as an employee to an employer. One thing is certain, if you don't have the vision to create financial wealth; someone else who has the vision will hire you to create his or hers. You actually need an entrepreneurial and investment mindset to be able to create financial wealth, not merely an employee mindset.

The truth is that employees only make their bosses rich; debtors make the banks rich; consumers make businesses rich; but investors only make themselves rich. And if you must be a successful investor, then don't invest your money or earnings in a bank account. That's an option for those who wants to be savers not investors. Hear what *Warren Buffet* said about this, *"banks are the legal thieves of the 21st century…they take your money, run businesses with it and give you stipends as dividends…"*.

You must wake up from your financial sleep to commit yourself to the wealth creation task of exploring and evaluating new investment opportunities in order for you to continue to invest your income earnings until you become financially independent, abundant and able to provide yourself with the basic needs of life including food, shelter, clothing, and comfort facilities; to acquire assets, property and or make diversified entrepreneurial business investments for diversified sources of income earning; to positively impact financially on the lives of others in need. Else if you ignore the wealth creation task only to continue with your financial sleep, *"how can you compete in a world where billionaires sleep for 5hours and they own the buildings where you pay rent and sleep for 10hours...think like a billionaire"* – Donald Trump.

Financial wealth creators who became hirer of labor

ALIKO DANGOTE:

This is an African man that rose from a modest beginning as a trader who as at the year 2017 has become the world's richest black man in Africa, sitting atop the biggest and most diversified conglomerates in Africa. The way he started has continued to challenge and inspire his friends and foes alike, for here is a man who started out modestly as a commodity trader under his uncle but has today, by dint of raw doggedness with hard work, single-handedly built the biggest quoted and most diversified conglomerate in Africa. Like the Biblical mustard seed, the NGN500,000 naira loan that Dangote took from his uncle to start trading in rice, sugar and cement has transformed the business with physical presence in over 14 African countries. Today, he ranks among the world's billionaires by Forbes magazine, with a personal fortune estimated at 11.2 billion Dollars as at 2016.

SIR RICHARD BRANSON:

For gold to come out refined it is passed through the fire; so for a millionaire in the making to emerge a world changer, there must be room for personal development. Sir Richard Branson (KBE) is a flamboyant British entrepreneur with a seemingly insatiable appetite for starting new businesses. His internationally recognized brand "Virgin" is splashed across everything from credit cards to airline and music "mega stores". Branson continuously seeks new business opportunities and loves a good challenge, especially when he enters a market that is dominated by a few major players. Richard Branson was born on July 18, 1950. His entrepreneurial ways began early when he was publishing a student magazine at the age of 16. Branson did not go on to graduate from school, but in 1970 the now famous Virgin brand had its beginning in the form of a discount records mall order venture that he and his friend Nik Powell worded on.

By the early 1980's, Virgin Records was one of the top six record companies in the world. Then, in 1984, Branson got a phone call out of the blues suggesting a Jumbo Jet passenger service between London and New York. Branson liked the idea, much to the horror of his fellow directors who thought him crazy. Undeterred, he announced to the world that Virgin Atlantic Airways would begin operating within three months! An aircraft was found, staff were hired, license granted and, thanks in no small part to Branson's infectious enthusiasm. On June 22, 1984, an aircraft packed with friends, celebrities and the media set off for Newark, New Jersey – and a phenomenon was born. The airline was founded on the concept of offering competitive and high quality first class and economy services. The airline holds many major airline awards and recently earned "Airline of the year Award" for the third consecutive time.

Since 1985, Richard has actively engaged in his vocations and been involved in a number of record-breaking land, air speed and distance attempts. In 1986, his boat, "Virgin Atlantic Challenger II," rekindled the spirit of the Blue Riband by crossing the Atlantic Ocean in the fastest recorded time ever. In 1993, the combined sales of Virgin Group companies exceeded $1 billion in United States. In addition to his own business activities, Branson is a trustee of several charities, including The Healthcare Foundation, a leading healthcare charity responsible for the launch of a health education campaign named Parents Against Tobacco (PAT), whose aim is to limit tobacco advertisements and sponsorship in spots. In December 1999, Branson signed an agreement to sell a 49% stake of Virgin Atlantic to Singapore Airlines to form a unique global partnership. It turned out that 1999 was an eventful year for Branson, topped off by his being awarded a knighthood for his services to entrepreneurship. Richard lives in London and Oxford-shire and is married with two children.

The story goes on..., quite a life! As you might imagine, Branson never stops (which can be exhausting for the people around him!) What a genius! Here is someone who worked on his skills and properly packaged himself in order to make the outstanding impact he has made. It is passion that keeps a man running with each breaking day. Friends, Branson's passion propelled him as he built himself in order to stand in the middle of his dreams. Albert Einstein said; "the significant problems we face cannot be solved at the same level we were when we created it". It is time to develop yourself. Look within you and harness those gifts in you. Build your skills so as to become relevant to our world. Process your raw materials for greatness: your own talents and confidence. Richard Branson wants Virgin to be as well known around the world as Coca-Cola.

HENRY J. HEINZ: Perhaps you are a woman and you make vegetable meals (salad) often, then I am sure you are a regular user of Heinz salad cream. Are you a student or you can still remember your secondary school days when "baked beans" was common? Then you must have eaten Heinz baked beans. Are you a regular user of tomato ketchup? If you are, then you must be familiar with Heinz tomato ketchup. Even on the scanty shelves of super markets in rural areas, the food brands of Henry J. Heinz, an American who died almost 100 years ago are still being displayed for sales. I tell you, this is something remarkable. Henry J. Heinz is known by some as the founder of the largest food empire in the world, but I call him the food specialist. Even in this century, it will not generate controversy if I call him the greatest food industrialist this world has ever known. The eldest son of a family of German immigrants was he. Ten years old was he when his gardening activities led to his selling a wheelbarrow full of vegetables round the village of his upbringing (Sharpsburg, east of Pittsburgh, Pennsylvania) every day, and at twelve he was growing enough to load a horse and a cart. In 1869, at the age of twenty-five, he incorporated HENRY J. HEINZ FOOD firm.

H. J. Heinz was one of the first American companies to introduce staff welfare facilities. The founder (Henry J. Heinz) insisted that the firm provided staff with dining room, locker rooms, dressing rooms, gymnasia, swimming pools, uniforms, free medical treatment, free life insurance and further education. Henry was not just out to make money but had the welfare of his workers at heart. At the time of Henry's death, H.J. Heinz food firm had 6,523 employees, 26 factories, 227 offices and other premises and 100,000 acres of farmland. Whaoo! What foot prints to leave on the sands of time! But hold on, what was the core value of his life?

'The real passion of life', said the Dean of Pittsburg University, 'was his religion.' Henry J. Heinz made it very clear what he meant religion when he prefaced his own last will and testament with these words" *'Looking forward to the time when my earthly career shall end, I desire to set forth at the very beginning of this will as the most important item in it, confession of my Father Jesus Christ as my Saviour'*. Such was the foundation of Henry J. Heinz's life's success. In the midst of overflowing wealth, the greatest value of his life was relationship with the Lord Jesus Christ. After reading this eye opener on the life of a great man who walked in success that outlived him, the million-dollar question to ask is 'What is the foundation of my own life?' Do you think you know so much? Do you think you have money and so cannot serve the Lord Jesus (or do you fear a life of penury in serving God)? Then meditate again on the life of Henry J. and see that it is God that gives power to make wealth. The summary of it all is that Jesus Christ is the foundation of lasting success, and you need Him in your life now. I mean right now.

JOHN D. ROCKER FELER:

For every glory, there is a corresponding story. Tough times never last but tough people do. John D Rockefeller was born on July 8, 1839 in Richford, New York about midway between Binghamton and Ithaca. His father, William Avery Rockefeller, was a "pitchman", a "Doctor" who claimed he could cure cancers and charged up to $25 per treatment. He was gone for months at a time travelling around the west from town to town and would return to wherever the family was living with substantial sums of cash. His mother Eliza Davison Rockefeller was very religious and disciplined. She taught John to work, save, and give to charities.

On September 26, 1855, he got a job as assistant book keeper with Hewitt & Tuttle, commission merchants and produce shippers. He was very exacting and scrupulously honest. For example, he would not write out a false bill of lading under any circumstances. He went to great lengths to collect overdue accounts. He was pleasant, persistent, and patient and he got the company's money from delinquents (for all this work, he was not paid; but whatever he was paid, he always gave to his church and local charities). On March 1859, several months before his 20th birthday, Rockefeller went into business for himself, forming partnership with a neighbor, Maurice Clark. Each man put up $200 and formed Clark and Rockefeller Commission merchants in grain, hay, meats, and miscellaneous goods. At the end of the first year of the business, they had grossed $450,000, making a profit of $4400 in 1860 and $17,000 in 1861.

The commission merchant business was very competitive and Clark & Rockefeller's success was due in large part to Rockefeller's natural business abilities. Rockefeller's style was very precise and calculated. He was not a gambler but a planner. He avoided speculation and refused to work extremely hard. Rockefeller began investigating the feasibility of entering the oil refining business in 1862 and the firm of Andrews, Clark and company was formed in 1863. Rockefeller abhorred waste and devoted considerable energy to increasing the efficiency of its refining business. He believed that the secret of success was 'attention to detail'. In 1866, John D. brought his brother William Rockefeller into the partnership and they built another refinery in Cleveland which they named the

Standard Works. They also opened a New York office with William Rockefeller in charge to handle the export business which eventually became larger than the domestic business. In 1867, Henry M. Flagler (1830-1913) became a partner hence, Rockefeller, Andrews and Flagler was formed.

Flagler and Rockefeller were very much alike-ambitious and shrewd, with a taste for expansion. Investments made into the company were used to expand the company further and by 1868, Rockefeller, Andrews & Flagler were the largest refiner in the world. Flagler and Rockefeller understood that the only way to make profit consistently in oil refining was to make the business as large as possible and utilize all their 'waste' products. In short, nothing was left to chance, nothing was guessed at, and nothing was left unaccounted and unmeasured. Efficiencies down to the smallest detail of the business were the order of the day.

Economy, precision, and foresight were the cornerstones of their success. What a legend! O boy! I almost feel like this is tales by moonlight, but no! It's real! And we have an opportunity to learn from this great man who above all, had his foundation in Christ. The Rockefeller family is known internationally as a tithing family (tithe is a tenth of all your income, given to God in obedience to His divine command). Observing that John D. was engaged in various acts of giving and philanthropy because he understood that, for there to be a constant supply of his income, he needed to create a channel as he released that which he had, the law of multiplication sets in. Your business is waiting for you to adopt this principle of giving so as to open more doors of expansion.

CHAPTER FIFTEEN

THE OTHER SIDE OF THE COIN OF FINANCIAL WEALTH

Multiply your financial wealth

God has given you and me the self-will to be partakers of His instituted manifold giving. God did not only institute manifold giving but also became the first ever to demonstrate and practice giving through His magnanimous and generous offering of His only begotten Son, Jesus Christ in whom we have now through faith received the prosperity of financial wealth to live in riches. Therefore, if you want to multiply your financial wealth, you must also be a partaking-covenant giver both to God and fellow men. Hear this, investment can only diversify and increase your income but it takes giving to multiply your income by the rewarding hand of divinity. Of course, multiplying financial wealth through the act of giving is a universal principle that works for whosoever that keys into it, regardless of religion. It doesn't matter whether you a Christian or not.

For God so love the world that He gave… (John3v16). Behold I give you… (Luk.10v19). And He gave them… (Math.10v1). The manifold giving of God is this; that God in and through His only begotten Son, Jesus Christ gave man not only the fullness of His head but also the fullness of His divine Spirit nature by which man has become a partaker of His supreme authority with mighty power to make or create, own and possess financial wealth. And so, God wants you to give back to Him always from your financial wealth whether as a thanksgiving offering; as a sacrifice offering; as a free-will offering; as a first fruit offering *(Deut12v6)*; or as a tithe *(Gen.14v20, Mal.3v8-12, Math.23v23)*. Of course, you can make your giving either on a religious basis to support God's kingdom work or on a philanthropic basis to support charity or community development.

However, let me say here that how much you will be able to make riches or create, own and possess financial wealth is not in any way determined by whether you give much, less or not at all. It is not by giving that a man creates financial wealth. No! Even the most stingy man on earth can still create an enormous financial wealth in life so long as he gets himself involved into wealth creation process with strategic application of its principles. Nevertheless, by giving you can actually multiply your financial wealth, because the hand of divinity is always awaiting to reward you as a giver by bringing on your way more financial opportunities and open doors in order for you to reap a multiple fold of return on whatever you may have given out over a time towards either impacting on the society or making lives of others better and more meaningful. In other words, giving is optional in determining how much financial wealth that you can create, own and possess but it is a necessity not only for multiplying it but also for living in the same footsteps of God who did not spare His own Son, Jesus Christ, for He had freely with Him given us all things, include the very financial wealth that you are today owing, possessing, controlling and enjoying *(Rom.8v32)*.

Imagine what would have been our fate if Christ had not become poor for our sake that we might through Him by His grace become rich to be able to now create financial wealth. I guess we would have all faced the fate of the misery of poverty and penury. If God could and had through Christ freely made us to become partakers of His riches of financial wealth, you and I therefore must tow the same path of His exemplary steps to give back to Him in such ways as the Bible tells us to do.

"The silver is Mine, and the gold is Mine, Says the LORD of hosts. Bring all the tithes into the storehouse, That there may be food in My house, And try Me now in this, Says the LORD of hosts, If I will not open for you such blessing That there will not be room enough to receive it. Give and it will be given to you: good measure, pressed together, and running over will be put into your bosom. For with the same measure that you use, it will be measured back to you.

For you know the grace of our Lord Jesus Christ, that though He was rich, yet for your sakes He became poor, that you through His poverty might become rich. For I do not mean that others should be eased and you burdened; but by an equality, that now at this time your abundance may supply their lack, that their abundance also may supply your lack-that there may be equality. As it is written, He who gathered much had nothing left over, and he who gathered little had no lack.

But this I say: He who sow sparingly will also reap sparingly and he who sows bountifully will also reap bountifully. So let each one give as he purposes in his heart, not grudgingly or of necessity; for God loves a cheerful giver. And God is able to make all grace abound toward you, that you, always having all sufficiency in all things, may have abundance for every good work. Do not be deceived, God is not mocked; for whatever a man sows, that he will also reap..." *(Hag.2v8, Mal.3v10, Luk.6v38, 2Cor.8v9, 13-15, 9v6-8).*

The symbolic spiritual significance of why you should always be giving onto God or be a giver for God's sake is: to show your gratitude and express your appreciation of how grateful you are unto God for His daily mercies, goodness and blessings of provision, sustenance, deliverance and above all the redemption and salvation of your soul; to advance the course of humanity and God's kingdom on earth through the church; to renew God's covenant of fruitful multiplication for increase in your life; to fulfil the law of return to source (God) for a new release of higher measure in return *(Gen.22v1-2, 15-18, Luk.6v38, 2Cor.8v9)*; to fulfill the law of obedience to emulate the exemplary footsteps of our patriarchs of faith and God, our Creator as great givers *(2Sam.24v24, Acts10v2, Rom.8v32).*

To give or to be a giver is a covenant obligation for every child of God. Giving is inevitable if at all you want to multiply your financial wealth. *"... Give Me a drink" (John4v7).* Christ was actually asking the woman of Samaria to give Him water if she really wants to have inside of her a ceaseless flow of the spring of living water. If you want to have a ceaseless multiplying flow of financial wealth, then you equally have to cultivate the culture of giving. *Christ also says, "Give and it will be given to you..." - (Luk.6v38).* When you give, God multiplies what you have given and return it in the fold of good measure of financial wealth that is shaking together and pressed down which runs over. You may be rich before men but if you are excusing yourself from giving especially to impact and improve on the lives of others around you, then in God's sight you are poor not rich.

Rich before men, but poor in God's sight

There are men who are rich in financial wealth in terms of their size of money income, assets and business investments, yet they are poor because they are found wanting in doing deed of good-works. These categories of men are rich before men but they are poor in God's sight.

The untold truth is that the world today measures a man's financial wealth by their assets, businesses, investments and income returns accruing to them, but God measures a man's riches by the deed of good-works that he converted his riches into. Men who claim to be rich in financial wealth but has no evidence of deed of good-works to show are only rich before men but very poor in God's sight. It is not how great or excessively rich you are but how much of great or excessive good-works have you done to benefit others with your riches. You must actively invest your financial wealth into rendering impactful good-works towards the poor, the less privileged *(Deut.15v7-11, Math.25v34-40, Provb.19v17, Gal.6v9-10)*, and for the growth and advancement of God's kingdom work *(Luk.8v2-3, 12v48)*.

Of course, God has not sent you to achieve the prosperity of financial wealth only for your selfish living, competition and comparison with others of which most of the rich men and men of riches have always demonstrated by their luxury and affluent living as a way of showcasing their self-pride. The purpose for you to create, own and possess financial wealth shouldn't be to build a project of vanity here on earth but to build a project of legacy on earth and treasures in heaven.

Personally, investing my money to impact and improve on the lives of people especially the youths from the less privileged and poor families is a life time calling I have chosen to answer. Changing and bettering the lives of others with my financial wealth is the greatest thing I do that gives me inexpressible joy. To the glory of God and by His grace, I have a good number and still counting, of people whose destiny I have been able to shape and lives given a better meaning; who today have become my sons and daughters in the Lord. And I will continue to do more of this selfless sacrifice to leave an outliving life legacy.

Following man's choice to continue to live in bondage to the lie and deception of the mind about becoming rich, it has created an age longed system of human existence wherein the paupers and the poor or the less privileged wouldn't cease forever to live among the rich and the men of riches *(Lev.25v35, Deut.15v7-11)*. In other words, it won't be an overstatement to say that, beside every rich man there is always a dying pauper or poor man around him. Whenever you are deploying your financial wealth to make valuable impact in the society and in the lives of others, you are indeed laying up treasures that does not only has an eternal reward but also earns you financial favor from God that would enable you to reap financial miracles in folds *(Math.6v19-20, Luk.12v33)*.

Therefore, your financial ability can as well be measured in terms of the extent or level of impact you are making in your society and in the lives of the have 'nots' around you.

This is a key sacrifice that you shouldn't avoid to make in life as a rich person. The more you make more of this commendable selfless sacrifice in the society and in the lives of others, the more God will continue to multiply your financial wealth into higher measures *(Luk.6v38)*.

Moreover, your impact is required to be extended towards God's kingdom works. As a rich man or man of riches, you are expected to actively sponsor the work of the great commission and His other kingdom projects. At your discretion you may wish and choose either to do so or not. Nevertheless, it is divinely ideal to do so. Because to sponsor the work of the great commission and finance God's kingdom projects is indeed a universal divine call upon all men especially those who by God's grace have succeeded in creating financial wealth *(Neh.3v14-16, Luk.8v1-3)*.

Remember, you are not created by God to live for yourself only to actualize your personal visions and self-projects. You are equally living for God to sponsor the evangelization of the Gospel of Christ for the purpose of winning the dying soul of sinful men and to finance kingdom projects such as church buildings, equipping and furnishings of the church, welfare and humanitarian ministries of the church, etc. This kind of sponsorship and financing you can always do through your paying of tithe, giving of offerings, sowing of faith seeds, freewill donations and grants, other incidental financial support to the churches of God or to any independent gospel ministries closer or far to you. Meanwhile the paupers, the poor, the rich-poor, the rich and the men of riches all do have a chance within the limit of their respective financial ability to make a level of selfless sacrifices for the sake of others.

Yes, it is not evil in God's sight for you to use your financial wealth to build an empire of business, acquire assets of real estate, and to make other valuable investments, provided you are wisely using them to fulfilling a godly purpose. Even God once told prophet Jeremiah to invest in real estate and acquire landed property *(Jer.32v6-15)*. King Solomon too had diversified investments that were yielding returnable incomes to him *(1Kg.9v26-28, 2Chr.1v16-17, 9v21-22)*. Also, the scriptures says, *"So Jehoshaphat became increasingly powerful ... He had much property in the cities of Judah; ...Jehoshaphat had riches and honor in abundance..." (Chr.17v12-13, 18v1)*. Unfortunately, Satan has continued to mislead most of the rich men and men of riches to believe in error that the purpose of creating financial wealth is only for luxury and affluent living to showcase their self-pride.

God doesn't want man to showcase or display any atom of self-pride. But most of the rich men and men of riches by their luxury and affluent living have continued to express an ungodly nature of their self-pride. Is it not a luxury and affluence to showcase self-pride when all you could do as a rich man or man of riches is to build and acquire multiple assets of real estate and landed property here and there only for yourself, both within and outside the country, yet you can't even provide even the least kind of livable shelter for any of the poor and wretched families who are scattered everywhere around you, with some even homeless?

Is it not a luxury and affluence to showcase self-pride when all you could do as a rich man or man of riches is to continue to buy and park in your garage brand new of every latest model of cars, yet you can't even buy the cheapest of a new car or give out any of your used cars to the poor and wretched people around you? Is it not a luxury and affluence to showcase self-pride when all you could do as a rich man or man of riches is to continue to stock your various bank accounts with excessive money deposit, yet you can't even offer any free or unconditional financial help or assistance to the poor and wretched people around you?

Is it not a luxury and affluence to showcase self-pride when all you could do as a rich man or man of riches is to send to and train your children at the best available academic institutions, yet you can't even pay for the school fees of any of the children of the poor and wretched families around you? Is it not a luxury and affluence to showcase self-pride especially as a politician or public office holder when all you could do is to amass, embezzle and loot public fund or treasury only to build an empire of financial wealth from which you bribe or lobby the helpless poor voters and the high profile political cabals in order to immortalize your political office or stay in politics for life, yet you can't even seek for the wellbeing of the poor masses who voted you into office or consider their condition of poverty, suffering, hardship, pain which are consequent upon your heartless act of looting?

Is it not a luxury and affluence to showcase self-pride when all you could do as an overseer or superintendent of God's church is to build and acquire in your name all manner of assets and investments, live in a heaven on earth mansions, keep with you fleet of best of latest cars, and personal jets that even some states or nations can't afford, yet there are some of your members who will live in poverty for the rest of their life; who currently are unable to afford their basic needs of good food, clothing and shelter; without any hope to afford even the least of life-needing comfort; to acquire even a single assets or investment in their name let alone to ever live in their life to enjoy riches.

One may then ask, how do I mean? Does it mean that I am in anyway an advocate of poverty instead of riches?

No! I am not at all. Am only saying that most of the rich men and the men of riches are not actually fulfilling God's purpose for which He wants men to be so rich. In fact, whether you are a rich man or a man of riches as long as you are unwilling, not ready, and actively doing nothing for the sake of God's love to impact and improve on the lives of the poor people around you and to bring them up as possible as you can to live and enjoy with you the same quality and self-fulfilling life that you are living; then your luxury and affluent living is obviously nothing but a display and showcasing of self-pride over these poor people around you whom you selfishly does not want to be with you at the same pedestrian of luxury and affluent living. What a selfishness! Remember, whatever is the degree of your financial wealth, it makes no sense if you don't use them to reach out to give others a lifting hand in life.

This ugly reality alone has continued to widen the gap between the poor and the rich. Consequently resulting to a generational structure of capitalistic exploitation and imperialism by which the rich men and the men of riches have continued to selfishly enslave the poor and take undue advantage of their potentials to survive and become rich too. In this case, is it justifiable in God's sight? Sure, you will answer better. That is why you must as a rich man or a man of riches invest heavily in God's project by either giving to or providing for others especially the poor around you. By this way you will not only stand rich in God's sight but you will also find happiness in life.

Sustaining your financial wealth

To sustain financial wealth is much more difficult than to create it. If you fail to sustain financial wealth when created, you may end up losing all sooner than you wouldn't expect. Failing to understand this principle of sustaining financial wealth could be very daisy. Once you become an owner, possessor and controller of financial wealth, you are bound to face the sustainability test. This requires you to deal with the five armed-hackers of financial wealth; and if not handled well can gradually crash down your financial wealth and retire you to poverty. These five armed-hackers are: Pride of life Syndrome, Materialistic Obsession, Monetization Attitude, Euphoria Rest, Extravagant Spending Adventure, etc.

Pride of life syndrome is an attitude of bragging or boasting with your financial wealth, which sometimes may result to using them to intimidate or oppress others who are poor, or to support or fight in favor of evil, harmful, foolish or unjust cause *(1Tim.6v9)*. **Materialistic obsession** is a conscious attitude of dissatisfaction and greed to endlessly acquire financial wealth and increase riches at all cost by all means whether good or bad. It is an attitude of greedy consciousness to have everything at your possession which sometimes may lead you into committing certain crime, evil or wickedness *(1Tim.6v10)*.

Also, **monetization attitude** is an attitude of being money conscious with the erroneous idea that your money-riches can do everything for you in life. It is not true. The scripture said that money can answer all things but it never said it can do all things *(Ecc.10v19)*. For instance, money can answer to your health problems, say sickness, but it can't do anything to give life itself to you *(Luk.12v15)*. **Euphoria rest attitude** is a wrong attitude that leaves you with the perception that you have made it or arrived in making financial wealth after all, and now has to fold your hands just to rest in celebration and enjoyment of your riches *(Luk.12v16-21)*. **Extravagant spending adventure** is a self-oriented crazy drive or propensity to be spending wastefully and lavishly of a higher proportion of income returns from your financial wealth for just mere personal satisfaction and pleasures which could fast depreciate the stock of your financial wealth than you are creating it.

Many had once created financial wealth but couldn't sustain theirs, for they negligently allowed some of these armed-hackers to crash down their stock of financial wealth. And today they are no longer among the rich men or men of riches who are living at higher and extreme point of financial ability. Any man who allows any of these armed-hackers to crash down his financial wealth today would always live tomorrow to look for the same financial wealth that he had once created yesterday *(Ecc.10v6-7)*.

Your understanding of the purpose of creating financial wealth is the only reliable back-up program that can actually enable you to sustain yours. If you really want to escape these armed-hackers, then you will have to identify yourself with the wisdom of making use of your financial wealth to build a legacy of impact for the good of others. Otherwise you may not be lucky enough to continue for long to sustain your financial wealth. When you create financial wealth, it brings to you satisfaction, and prompt the world to celebrate you and heaven to rejoice with you.

However, the purpose for you to create, own and possess financial wealth is not: to be full of pride, to be materialistic Obsessed, to monetize everything in life, to be in euphoria rest to enjoy your riches, or to embark on extravagant spending adventure. You can sustain your financial wealth to immortalize it with a legacy that will live after you.

Financial liquidation

Just as there is financial miracle there is also what is called financial liquidation. As much as you can experience and enjoy financial miracle, you can equally experience and suffer financial liquidation. *Financial liquidation is the gradual self-process of folding up your finances and wealth until you are finally exposed to financial starvation and landed into poverty through your indulgence in bad financial lifestyle and habit of excessive borrowing, competitive or comparative spending, advance spending, extravagant spending, and unsecured lending than your current overall income can adequately accommodate.* Sometimes, financial liquidation if not immediately checked and controlled may land you into a life time financial starvation and poverty. It is very obvious that financial liquidation is a factor of excessive borrowing, competitive or comparative spending, advance spending, and or extravagant spending that has gotten out of the reach and coverage of your current income.

Hear this if you really want to escape the web of financial liquidation. You can actually borrow when it has only become necessary. But disengage yourself henceforth from any borrowing that is in excess far more above your income. Don't borrow any money that you cannot repay from your income within the shortest possible time. Endeavor to live a debt free life. What you can't pay cash for is not your size. Don't lend out unsecured money that you can't part with as gift should there be any default, so that you don't jeopardize your business or relationship.

Also, spending is good. Because we all work hard to earn money; and we all live to spend money. But ensure that you discourage yourself from comparative or competitive spending. Don't compare or compete yourself with another person in spending. If you buy things you do not need, soon you will have to sell things you need which you already have.

You don't need to compare or compete yourself with other persons on how they or you are spending. You don't need such comparison of spending for you to measure whom you are better off or who has a lesser level of financial ability than you in life. Never should you engage in advance spending before or ahead of getting your income. Nor should you live with the habit of extravagant spending. It is extravagant and irrational for you to spend on things that not for immediate need. Do not save what is left after spending, but spend what is left after saving. Don't spend recklessly, unwisely or wastefully on frivolities or on things that are not necessities, important, useful, needful, priorities in most cases like pleasures. *"He who loves pleasures will be a poor man; and he who loves wine and oil will not be rich" (Prb.21v17).* If you can heed to all the above cautions you will definitely escape financial liquidation.

Warning over riches and those who own and possess financial wealth

In as much as creating, owning and possessing financial wealth as a dimension of prosperity is not evil; yet you should not in the bid, struggle and quest for it either allow devil to lead you into any of these evil act, wickedness, atrocity such as assassinating, kidnapping, fraud, robbery or stealing, sabotaging, as a means of making money. It is not worth doing at all. Because, *"as a partridge that broods but does not hatch, so is he who gets riches, but not by right; it will leave him in the midst of his days, and at his end he will be a fool"* *(Jer.17v11)*. No matter your quest for riches, never should you seek to create financial wealth under the shade of any sharp practice nor through exploitative or imperial capitalism. If you do, it will be judged against you before God as a mark of selfish interest to the detriment of both your victims and the economy.

That you had passed through the wilderness of emptiness, contention, suffering, abuse, opposition and or battle before eventually succeeding in becoming an owner and possessor of financial wealth should never be a reason at all for you to shut the door of your riches against the poor nor choose to be selfish and exploitative of other people around you. Life is all about sacrifices you make in good conscience. Of course, sacrifices do not count costs but are made free of charge from the gains that God's grace upon your life has made possible for you to make. God having allowed His son to become poor for your sake had made the greatest sacrifices for you to be able to create and own financial wealth. And so you too ought to make same to help others succeed in life.

Besides, you must not seek to pursue to create and own financial wealth with the spirit of greed and covetousness.

Rather your pursuit to be rich in life should be with a balanced spirit and attitude of contentment. Even God Himself as the king of the heavenly kingdom and the kingdom of the entire universe is content with all that He had created *(Gen.1v31)*. Had He not been content, He would have desired to create more things for Himself since He has the power to do so. The attitude of contentment in God in relation to financial wealth ownership and possession should always be; to be content at present with whatever financial wealth you have created that is currently determining your money income, but still trusting God with a hope for more of them tomorrow, while you go on today working hard and taking necessary actions toward creating more of financial wealth in order to own and possess more money income that you still desire. Just like Paul, we must live and abide by this God's accepted standard *(Ph.4v13, 1Tim.6v6)*.

The word of God warns thus, "... *if riches increases do not set your heart on them*" *(Ps.62v10)*. No matter how fast or in folds that your financial wealth is increasing, don't succumb to the temptation of setting your heart on it. And never you be too money conscious to be a slave to it or to serve it as an idol instead of it serving you as its owner; and as a means not as an end. Create, own and possess financial wealth and live a rich life as long as you have the opportunity through any means that is acceptable and pleasing to God; but never should you love riches nor let it to be your enslaving master leading you to engage or indulge into all manner of evil. When you love riches, you become insatiable of financial wealth; and this has with the trait to cause you sleepless night that could expose and lead you to evil thought on how to become an owner and possessor of it at all cost by all means, even when it seems to be evil.

Yet don't be over spiritual to regard money as a worthless carnal possession. You should better see it as a needful means of exchange that will enable you while here on earth to do a whole lot of things needful for you to fulfill your destiny. So long as you live on earth you can't escape this all important exchange process. Perhaps you don't know, God is God of exchange who from the beginning of times had always continued to use His "Word" as a divine tender to buy and secure whatever He had ever wanted to create for everlasting possession *(Gen.1v3, John3v16, 1Cor.6v20, 2Cor.8v9)*.

However, be careful to love God than to love money with riches that it brings. *For riches are not forever ... (Prb.27v24)*, but God is. When you love money with the riches that it brings than God, it can become root of evil in your life *(1Tim.6v10)*. In this world, you are to love God than money. You are not to trust in your financial wealth nor in anything else whatsoever that you can buy, secure or acquire by money for *he who trusts in his riches fail but the righteous will flourish like foliage (Prb.11v28)*. Rather, you are to trust in the living God to not only give you the power to make or create financial wealth but also to give you grace to be rich in good works, in giving and in sharing with others *(1Tim.6v9-10, 17-19)*.

Here this, *"will you set your eyes on that which is not? For riches certainly make themselves wings; they fly away like an eagle toward heaven" (Prb.23v5)*. In essence the wise man Solomon is reminding whoever that cares that it takes you having God to fly upward with the power to make or create financial wealth in life. Without God you will struggle and labor in vain to create financial wealth let alone to become rich which are compared to as having wings like an eagle to fly far away from you toward heaven. In other words, you really need God who dwells in the heavenly abode into whose hands all riches fly, to release downward onto you all of the financial wealth you desire in life to create.

ABOUT THE AUTHOR

Anthony Cepman A. O., is an anointed Man of God gifted with dimensions of apostolic grace, a charismatic preaching-Teacher and Evangelist, a Prophet of restoration, a passionate Humanitarian crusader, an Entrepreneur and business investment manager, an Administrator and Management practitioner, a Marriage counsellor and therapist, a renowned Author of bestselling books as well as a motivational guest Speaker.

He is the vision Co-founder and global Coordinator of LIFE CHANGING MISSIONS INTERNATIONAL, a non-governmental Christian organization with a global charity-mission to Save Lives, Empower People especially the less privileged and to Shape Destinies of many, for a better living.

Also, he is married to Victoria and the marriage is graciously blessed.

Anthony Cepman A. O.

Email: tonybuchi@lifechangingmissionsintl.org

tonycepman@gmail.com

Website: www.lifechangingmissionsintl.org

www.ingramcontent.com/pod-product-compliance
Lightning Source LLC
Chambersburg PA
CBHW020631220526
45464CB00001B/99